AROUND *the* WORLD
IN 93 YEARS

An Uncharted Journey

Sue Dabney Catalano

ISBN: 978-1-4834-5701-7 (sc)
ISBN: 978-1-4834-5700-0 (hc)
ISBN: 978-1-4834-5702-4 (e)

Library of Congress Control Number: 2016913349

Cover painting by Christine Curry Coates
CCpainter.com

Lulu Publishing Services rev. date: 10/14/2016

Dedication

To my Navigator
who has steered me through life
to safe harbor.

Our Log

Preface

*T*he inspiration for this book comes directly from three women: the children Bob and I were privileged to have. They have filled my heart to the brim and will always reside there. They are the three parts of my heart.

Nina was our first baby, born in 1945. Bob didn't return from service in the Pacific until she was nine months old. Mother helped me through the pregnancy and Nina's first year; the bond we three formed during her infancy would never be broken. Nina held firm and loyal to her faith in God, withstanding misunderstanding in marriage and bearing with grace and character a prolonged bout with cancer. This was her cross to bear and dreadfully sad for us all. We had to say good-bye to her in 2005. Oh, how she delighted in her four children and her grandchildren! They were her reward and joy—and continue to be mine.

Nancy came next. She is an angel, confident and capable, with a tender, helping heart for each problem that comes her way. From her nursing and psychology training and experience, she has knowledge to solve problems in a sweet, gracious manner. Family, friends, and children of all ages run to her for help and solace; always they are met with compassionate understanding. She has been my anchor since Bob's passing, unshakable and ever dependable. I admire greatly how she and her husband, Gary, have raised their four children, who, while each on diverse career paths, radiate the fine qualities of their parents. The world is sure to be a better place for their talents. How it stirs me to see the great-grands—each a blessing.

Debby is our youngest. I believe she may well be responsible for my retaining a sense of humor, which has stood me in good stead through the steep path of my senior years. Bubbly Debby stands by her principles and commitments with determined strength and character— always with exceptional understanding and love of God. She shares my conviction that her six children, and now their children, are each a direct gift from God. They are her treasures—as well as mine. She is a multitalented woman with a giant heart. I appreciate deeply her loyalty and thoughtful consideration of me.

These three strong women are the fruit of my life. We have laughed, talked, and prayed together during the good as well as the hard times, bearing the latter more lightly because of each other. I feel my own mother must know and rejoice with me.

From my retirement home in Redlands, California, I have had the blessing of health and the luxury of time to reflect upon my extraordinarily full life of ninety-three years. I was beginning to hear my older grandchildren ask more and more questions about my experiences—they know only bits and pieces. I realized my answers could not be contained in conversations or short writings and began to ask myself if my story could be told in book form.

What a daunting idea! Impossible!

However, I had to admit to the importance of their knowing their roots, their place in history. It began to dawn on me that it would actually be selfish not to undertake the project, as hard as it might be to revisit some of the darker periods of my life.

Slowly it took hold that this was the time—the time to entrust my memories and my perspective to my girls and their children and their children's children. It would be my gift.

I felt the nudge of the Holy Spirit and heard the assurance of strength and guidance in this endeavor of love—love for my family and my country—so that future generations may understand what we have gone through to preserve freedom in our world.

Acknowledgments

*T*his book of memories that I dreamed of writing for my children, and theirs, could never have come to be had it not been for my very good and dear friend, Ariel Hollender. She calls herself a scribe—and that she is so talented to be. But she is much more to me.

She is always available to listen. We seem to be on the same spiritual plane, able to share our hearts and depend upon and listen for God's direction. As a result, she has been a true collaborator, understanding and helping me to organize and express my thoughts and experiences.

Teaming up with us has been my amazing, steadfast daughter and friend, Nancy. Her organizational and business skills in dealing with editing and publishing have been invaluable to me. Thanks for always being there for me, Nance!

I thank them, and I thank God for guiding us through our project to completion.

Introduction

*A*t no point in my life can I say I purposefully charted a course with goals in mind. Rather, it seemed that world events outside of my control determined my course. Even choices such as to travel to far-off shores were propelled by the times during which we lived.

I was on an uncharted journey. While that left me feeling lost at sea at times, my life was charged with excitement.

Then one day a sweet, miraculous knowing entered my soul, revealing that all along there had been a far stronger force than the events of the times affecting my journey. By grace, I understood the reality of a personal God, loving and protecting me. It was then I made a conscious choice that would transform me forever.

As I look back over my years and share them with you here, it is with opened eyes. In these pages you will find history from a personal perspective. It is also my hope that you will find inspiration, encouragement, and even some shared memories.

Chapter 1

Hollywood

Our Little World of Make-Believe

*T*here is someone I would like you to know—my mother, Marie Nolan Frizzelle. She was born in New York in 1887 of 100-percent Irish parents. Strong yet gentle, she was a lovely, lighted-hearted, well-read, intelligent, principled lady.

When she was young, Mother was the belle of the ball—pretty and vivacious, with plenty of beaus. One was Art, a fun-loving, Irish attorney-to-be, who fell completely in love and asked her to marry him. She delayed her response to him because she pictured marrying a more mature, aristocratic gentleman like Charles.

Art made a promise to call her a year from the date he'd proposed. If she had changed her mind about Charles, he would ask her again. Sure enough, exactly one year later Art did call—only to learn she had chosen Charles. Art was devastated but eventually did marry someone else.

Charles Frizzelle was twenty-three years her senior, a widower, with a son and daughter in their teens. He was born and grew up in West Waterville, Maine, and was of English, Scotch, French, and American-Indian heritage. His first wife had become ill with tuberculosis when their children, Christine and Morrill, were young. It was recommended that they move to a more suitable climate, so Charles relocated his optometry practice to downtown Los Angeles on Spring Street. After a few short years, his wife succumbed to the debilitating illness.

Upon her marriage to Charles, Mother entered his established household on Lorraine Boulevard. Of Dad's two children, it was Christine who resented the young wife's intrusion, and tried to influence her dad to side against Marie in all matters.

In spite of the difficulties with the first Frizzelle children, Mother's passion was to have children of her own, especially a daughter. Soon after marrying Charles she had her wish, but tragically the baby girl, Nina Marie, was stillborn.

The doctor admonished Mother to have no more children, but she ignored him and soon had a healthy baby boy. She gave him her family name, Nolan. Her initial disappointment at having a boy was fleeting as Nolan became her great joy. Determined again, in spite of the doctor's warning, she soon set about to have that baby girl. This time I arrived. It was August 3, 1923, two years after Nolan. Mother chose my name, thinking the double letters matched well—Suzzanne Frizzelle. Since that was long in itself, she added no middle name.

Inasmuch as there was the wide age difference between us and Dad's two older children, Nolan and I lived separate lives from them growing up. Eventually, though, after Chris was married with two children of her own, she and I genuinely began to enjoy each other's company. Nolan and Morrill later became good friends and golf buddies.

When Nolan and I were still very young, Dad and Mom decided to build a home in the Los Feliz area in Hollywood, near picturesque Ferndell and Griffith Park. The house was quite a remarkable place, designed by Frank Lloyd Wright and built by Paul Williams. Williams would soon achieve fame in his own right as an architect. He became a favorite of Hollywood celebrities, designing many elegant residences, as well as significant public buildings—the LAX theme building being only one example. And he did it as a pioneer: Paul Williams was African-American.

One day, years later, I was persuaded to take several family members to investigate my childhood home—I didn't need too much coaxing. We started out at the Beverly Hills Hotel, drove east to the Los Feliz area, and found 2134 E. Live Oak Drive. Thinking no one was at home, we peeked over the high hedge to take a look and were most embarrassed when the new owner came out to see if he could help us. However, after hearing why we were there, he gladly invited us in for a full tour. He was restoring the home's interior to its original state, so he was delighted to meet us and fascinated by my tales of the history of the house, as they added a personal richness to the research he had already done.

That house fit Mother well for she had natural social ease and grace. Still today when I see lavish parties depicted in old movies, my mind replays the scenes that Nolan and I witnessed as little children from the stairway, where we perched to peer down through the railing to the large rooms below. The women wore glamorous gowns; the men were elegant in their tuxes and ties. This part the movies always seemed to get right. From the sights and sounds of the music, dancing, and laughter, it looked to us as though being grown up might just possibly be as much fun as being kids.

In the 1920s in Los Angeles, the contemporary society of our parents and our elders was flourishing. Everyone seemed to be enjoying a fabulously prosperous, colorful, almost heady gaiety.

Nolan and I lived within that safe cocoon in a carefree, innocent world of our own.

The Roaring Twenties is a term sometimes used to refer to the 1920s, characterizing the era's distinctive cultural edge in most of the world's major cities for a period of sustained economic prosperity. Jazz music blossomed, the flapper redefined modern womanhood, and Art Deco peaked. Economically, the era saw the large-scale diffusion and use of automobiles, telephones, motion pictures, and electricity. The media focused on celebrities, especially sports heroes and movie stars....The social and cultural features known as the Roaring Twenties began in leading metropolitan centers, especially Chicago, New Orleans, Los Angeles, New York City, Philadelphia, Paris and London, then spread widely in the aftermath of World War I.

—Wikipedia

I didn't think twice about the practical aspects of our life then, but now, some ninety years later, I get a kick out of realizing how different it would look to you. Of course, we had no modern appliances such as dishwashers or even refrigerators. We had an icebox that held a fifteen-pound block of ice that was regularly delivered to the house by a horse-drawn wagon. Instead of a dryer, our washing machine had a wringer contraption on it that the clothes were hand-coaxed through prior to being hung on the outdoor clotheslines. A handy laundry chute went from way upstairs on the third floor to the wash room on the ground floor. Nolan and I often mischievously dared each other to slide down that chute—a wonderfully scary thought, but definitely and officially off limits.

Our school in Hollywood was Cheremoya, over one mile away (which seemed like four to me) down a steep hill to Franklin Avenue. We walked there most of the time, and Uncle Mac, Mother's sister Sabina's husband, usually picked us up after school. He was in the real estate business with an office close by.

My memories of early school are less vivid than our playtimes at home and in our neighborhood. Since we had no TV, computers, Disney parks, or the many other amusements that are yours today, our own imaginations had full reign. I wouldn't trade the experience, and, I daresay, Nolan felt the same way.

We made go-cart contraptions out of boards and roller skates, adding ropes to the front axle board for steering. Each of us had our own model and raced them down the hills of our front yard. We also played with our toy car and truck collection in the expansive dirt lot next door that became an elaborate car park, complete with intricate tunnels, roadways, and bridges.

And, oh my, the tree houses we built! They were havens never invaded by adults as they were accessible only by ropes and the ladders we made. I gave elaborate tea parties there for make-believe guests, the only real one being a rather awkward brother. Although, I must say, he was a good sport.

Being enterprising, we started a corner business. Across from us on Los Feliz Boulevard were splendid, multicolored flower fields cultivated by Japanese families who had settled in the area. They seemed to turn a blind eye to the buckets of blooms we surreptitiously gathered to sell at our homemade lemonade stand. We were proud of our success, learning later that Mother had been our discreet agent, prevailing upon her friends to patronize us.

When I wasn't playing with Nolan, I contented myself on our front porch, where I could easily spend hours with my magical dollhouses. That pleased our maid of the day, for she could keep better track of me there. Seems to me, we had a parade of maids. I remember only one clearly, a Miss Kirk, perhaps because she was the one who best fit the storybook stereotype of the English, straight-laced, pursed-lipped nanny. The cost of a maid was reasonable; Mother paid her twenty dollars per month and provided room and board.

It's hard for me to imagine a happier childhood than Nolan and I shared. Luckily, we were best friends, because no other young children lived nearby. I have always been grateful that Nolan tolerated his scrubby little sister. I loved him so.

With all the strength and resolve of his father's New England heritage, Dad loved us all and his young bride with her twinkling Irish joy. In his private life, he was a gifted pianist, composer, and romantic lyricist. Mother was his inspiration. Music at home in those days was an integral part of family life, and Dad's talent brought a memorable soundtrack to our childhood. Later on, when I was going to be married, Dad reached out tenderly to me, writing songs of love.

On most Sundays all four of us went hiking on the trails from Ferndell to the promontory point overlooking Los Angeles. That spot would later become the site of the Griffith Park Observatory, popular today with sightseers.

Mother sometimes grew reflective on those walks. At times I can still hear her voice echoing protectively, "Enjoy these precious childhood years and dreams," she'd say. "Adult problems will come soon enough." She had a way of expressing her wisdom in a practical manner, making the principles easy for us to absorb. Hers was a powerful love; it was the soil that gave us roots and lots of room to grow.

That tranquil life style would soon come to an abrupt end.

Chapter 2

Beverly Hills

Pre-Glamour, Quiet Town

So insulated were Nolan and I in our childhood world at our ages of eight and six that even the loud Crash of 1929 could not distract us. What did get our attention, however, was the need to move away from our accustomed, enchanted land of Los Feliz.

The Wall Street Crash and the Great Depression that followed began in late October 1929 and was the most catastrophic stock market crash in the history of the United States.

> The crash signaled the beginning of the 10-year Great Depression that affected all Western industrialized countries and did not end in the United States until the onset of American mobilization for World War II at the end of 1941.
>
> *—Wikipedia*

Dad had been buying on margin in the stock market. Consequently, he lost all his investments, was forced to declare bankruptcy, and had no choice but to watch helplessly as the Bank of America took over our house. Because Dad could not now purchase a house in his name, Mother wisely arranged for a loan in her father's name, Peter Nolan. While Grandfather Nolan was a moderately successful real estate broker, his son, Ed, was a well-respected lawyer in Los Angeles. It was Uncle Ed to whom Mother turned for that advice.

In 1932 we moved to our new home in Beverly Hills at 713 Canon Drive. Fatty Arbuckle, a well-known comedian in the early movies, had commissioned it to be built, but he had never lived there. That house remained our family home and focal point for gatherings large and small until Mother's death in 1947.

There was quite a bit of drama in our family surrounding the financial crisis, but as kids we were unaware. It was some years later before we began to grasp the details.

Uncle Ed was the CEO on the board of the Bank of Italy. Banks were starting to fold left and right, but the weight of the Depression had not yet been grasped. In an effort to try to save the Bank of Italy, Uncle Ed and many others on the board of directors sank their own money into it. Unbeknownst to them, A. P. Giannini, a director, had been negotiating a merge with the very young Bank of America. Soon the Bank of Italy was no more.

Uncle Ed lost absolutely everything; however, he was married to Grace Morse, a beautiful, regal, silent movie star with wealth of her own. She was a glamorous match for him. They lived in grand style at the Talmage Apartments on Wilshire Boulevard.

Ed's marriage to Grace held endless fascination for us kids, but I suspect she must have had a difficult time with Mother and her three sisters, Kit, Sabina, and Margaret. Nobody could be good enough for their adored brother. Telephones were an attraction in those days and the main avenue for their chatter. There were almost daily calls to each other to talk about family and the news. They relished lively exchanges of opinions, especially after reading humorist Will Rogers's earthy articles. His commentary on current events was a reliable guarantee of controversial banter.

After Ed recovered from the bank fiasco, he and Grace moved to Houston, Texas. This was at the time of the initial oil strikes, and he made another fortune. Many years later, when I noticed that we had not heard from Auntie Grace in some time, I called Uncle Ed's secretary, Miss Lee, to inquire about them. To my utter surprise, she told me he had passed away many months before. His premature death was shock enough, but intensifying our loss was the fact that we had not been notified.

Uncle Ed had made known his intention to leave half of his wealth to his family and half to Grace. We soon found out that prior to his death, his will had been rewritten— all in her favor. In short, Aunt Grace received everything, including a great deal of Exxon and other stocks, as well as family treasures. What's more, she had arranged his burial in the Court of Honor at Forest Lawn close by, yet our family had been told nothing.

She simply vanished from our lives—we assumed back to her original home in Boston. Aunt Grace's actions were sad and startling, to say the least. But I like to think that, in the end, her actions taught me at an early age of the hurt caused by greedy actions and that true value is not in possessions. This understanding has served me well through many losses.

When we moved to Beverly Hills, it was a quiet, respectable, village-like town. Mother and I often walked the many long blocks to visit Marion Hunter's bookstore. The sophisticated owners, Marion and Dick, became her friends as they shared discoveries in the pages surrounding them. While they chatted, I sat happily cross-legged on the floor, poring over beautifully illustrated books of all kinds.

Nolan's and my new school was Hawthorne Elementary. Our walk there with our new school chums was hardly dull; their insider information about the Hollywood lore all around us titillated our childish minds. On one corner of our block was the home of Harpo Marx with his grand, gold harp shining in the bay window. Across from Harpo's house was Jackie Cooper's, which was next to Tom May's home (of May Company).

From my upstairs window, I could look down into the tranquil garden of movie director Harry Lachman and his Chinese-American wife, Quon Tai. Being a young dreamer, I watched spellbound as the exotic, cheongsam-clad princess strolled along, chanting her singsong melodies. Maybe that was a prelude to my many wonderful encounters with Asian cultures in later years.

In contrast, our home life seemed ordinary, sedate, and—I thought at times—somewhat boring. Since Dad carried with him his deep, New England convictions of right and wrong, and because Mom embodied religious principles, they expected proper behavior. We were brought up honorably and conservatively in the straight and narrow tradition—but with a great deal of love and care. We were never subjected to arguments, shouting, or emotional episodes.

Dad was a complex man who loved his little family in his own way. He was the predictable workaholic, sidestepping family vacation plans with "I've got to keep my nose to the grindstone." Through his music, he expressed his feelings. He got and gave much enjoyment by plunking away on his piano late at night. On Sunday mornings when we were youngsters, he held Nolan on one knee and me on the other and read with great drama and laughter the extensive, colorful funny papers. And all of us were intrigued by his horse-racing hobby, watching quietly as he avidly doped out likely winners on his daily racing form. His favorite horse of all time was Seabiscuit.

Mother and Dad liked to play cards. They taught us bridge at an early age, and we enjoyed friendly poker games together too. Our other entertainment was the radio; it was to us like TV and digital devices are today. We were magnetized to it for President Roosevelt's Fireside Chats every Sunday night. His theme of "Happy Days Are Here Again" was giving the country hope, in spite of the well-publicized breadlines and frequent suicides. Then there were the lighthearted radio diversions of Myrt and Marge, Amos and Andy, the Bickersons, George Burns and Gracie Allen, Ed Wynn, and others.

About seven years passed in details like the ones I've described. Life was predictable. Dad's optometry practice was well established, as was his routine. At the close of business each day, he would leave his office at Seventh and Spring Streets after calling home to let us know he was ready to be picked up. We would then meet him at the red trolley station in Beverly Hills. The world was safe, and we were even safer within our loving home. Then there was an event that to Nolan and me was nothing short of devastating.

I was thirteen when a second, private crash happened. One evening Mother, Nolan, and I were together, waiting for the usual end-of-workday call from Dad. When he rang, I watched Mother saying incredulously into the receiver, "What? What!" Slowly hanging up, she turned to us and repeated the words that Dad had just uttered to her: "'I'm not coming home tonight or ever.'"

She sat in shock. I cried inconsolably. And Nolan erupted, declaring loudly that he never wanted to see or talk to Dad again. He was furious.

After a time, Mother carefully and deliberately explained to us that Dad loved us dearly and that he needed us more than ever and that we must see him as much as he wished. She stressed the problems were strictly between them and did not involve us in any way. She literally pushed the three of us together, which was healing for us. Eventually we held no long-standing hurt or resentment toward Dad.

As we talked to each of them, Nolan and I began to realize that they both had valid reasons to live apart. We put together the pieces of the puzzle that had led up to this outburst. Their private difficulties actually dated back some ten years. It was because of their devotion to the family unit that they had agreed to remain under one roof. Finally it had simply been too hard for Dad to keep up the happy family image.

Later in life, Nolan and I appreciated Dad more and more. Nolan and he spent time playing golf together. My relationship with him showed me his depth; I remember him most as being absolutely trustworthy and kind.

From Mother's point of view, Dad's stoicism and inability to demonstrate his affection to her in the ways that were important to her crushed her spirit, which led her to be very critical of him. There was never a question that Dad loved her deeply; he just couldn't endure her fault-finding.

Had there been counselors then, perhaps their differences could have been resolved.

Acceptance of their choice to separate made it possible to move on, and our Canon Drive home became a mecca where our school friends were welcome to congregate. One of them, Nolan's closest friend at Beverly Hills High, was Bob Dabney. When I enrolled there too, Bob became like a second brother, and I was their kid sister.

At home I would listen to them, rascals both, talking about the girls they were dating. In turn, the girls would often seek to relate their sides of the stories to me. More often than not, I found myself rising to the boys' defense. It was not lost on me that many of the girls sought to ingratiate themselves to me in order to be introduced to them. Having such a handsome brother who had an equally good-looking friend was quite a status symbol.

Nolan graduated from Beverly Hills High in 1939. But I stayed there only for my freshman year, then changed to Marlborough School for Girls in Los Angeles. Today Marlborough stands as the oldest independent girls' school in Southern California. It is still exceptional—continuing to impart high standards in academics, leadership, self-reliance, respect, and community service.

Marlborough's motto, oft repeated, was "Remember who you are and what you represent." That motto was an important guideline for me then as well as later in life. I knew my actions needed to reflect high standards, out of respect for my family.

The fuller picture of me at that young age must include that it was not unusual to find myself battling internally with insecurities. In contrast to others around me, it seemed my inadequacies were many. I had complexes about my ungainly looks and my scholastic abilities. I was taller than most and heavier, with unmistakable acne, braces on my teeth, and uncontrollable hair.

To make it worse, I was just average at everything. My B and C grades in school were painstakingly achieved. I strived to reach the hard-to-attain B, only to be met by Mother asking me to strive for an A. But more than a high achiever, I felt Mother wanted a beautiful model of a daughter. I was convinced I had let her down horribly. I felt lesser-than in every way.

Of course, that was not true. She was my mother and mentor; I loved her deeply and she me—there's no doubt of that. What I have expressed here are the raw feelings of a young girl. As I matured, Mother and I grew to understand each other and became very close.

All through our childhood, summer vacations were Mother's domain. She planned and organized every facet to give us the very best opportunities to explore our world. She leased our Beverly Hills home for one month each summer and with the money rented a cabin for us either at the beach or in the mountains at Lake Arrowhead. In the early years, when Dad was still living with us, he would drive back and forth on the weekends to wherever we were in order to keep up his office hours.

"Beaching it," as we called it here in California, was a way of life. We were never happier than when basking in the sun, walking in the warm sand, body surfing the waves, wolfing down hamburgers and Cokes, picnicking by bonfires in the sand, jumping big boulders on a jetty, playing games on the colorful piers, or grunion fishing by moonlight. Lasting friendships were forged, and carefree was the spirit.

When we were in Playa del Rey, Mom often sat by the big front windows of the Westport Beach Club. This gave her a perfect vantage point from which to watch us at play. I didn't sense any fear from her, but I'm sure she must have worried for our safety as we spent hours in the water.

What a sport it was to body surf! There were no surfboards or boogie boards then. It was all about body surfing. We would swim out beyond the waves. Then, treading water, we'd wait patiently for the right one that promised the thrill of taking us with it all the way to shore. It was like being a fish—free and one with the wave.

We tumbled back onto the warm sand, our chilled bodies soaking in the sun, and compared notes about what we had done right or what we could do to improve our next wave ride. We slathered baby oil everywhere and daubed our noses with white zinc ointment—but it was pretty useless. Our skin still often burned to the point of blistering and peeling. I pay to this day with periodic visits to the dermatologist who removes my recurring skin cancers.

Writing my story has sent me into the recesses of old boxes. In one I ran across this school essay, dated September 24, 1938. I was fifteen. It was typed, and on it my teacher had written "good" with a plus sign attached.

Battling the Briny Deep

My cap was on securely. My bathing suit hung with dignity. My courage was high with determination, and so I started out to battle the briny deep.

Maybe it was true that the lifeguard rescued five other swimmers before me. Perhaps the riptide did carry them out. Suppose the waves were as high as houses. What was the difference?

These facts meant nothing to me. I was a good swimmer. And, oh yes, I once won a medal.

With all the grace one could possess I dived into the raging Pacific Ocean. I must admit I landed right on my face and clipped a rock with the top of my head, but I wasn't going to give up.

*Then there came a wave — a huge, choppy wave —
rolling up bigger and bigger. I tried and I tried to
reach it before it broke, but no, I didn't quite make
it. With tremendous force it crashed right on me.
Other waves would have passed on, but this one
wanted to batter the conceit out of me. And it did,
plus confidence and life.*

*It slapped me to the bottom, rolled me into shore,
and dragged me out again. A fellow riptide came
along and twirled me 'round and 'round. My luck
then came back and I was able to stagger to my feet.*

*With a rip in my bathing suit, cap off, and wet,
stringy hair, this subdued little nonentity managed
to reach the safety of the locker room.*

I chuckle at my teenage words, because they aptly capture
the essence of what I've been trying to describe. Like most
teens, I felt indestructible, even as I experienced the battering
of the waves and the power of the ocean.

Going to the mountains was equally as much fun as the
beaches. Lake Arrowhead is a beautiful, scenic area with
great boating. Howard Hughes had a place up there and
kept a Chris-Craft boat on the lake. He let Nolan and his
friends use it as much as they liked. Being a daredevil, he
liked fostering risk-taking in the boys. He also had great
faith in the boat's stability; he told them if they could make
it capsize, they could have it. Needless to say, Nolan and
Bob did everything in their power to challenge the boat.
The boat won.

One summer, in the wooded mountains of Arrowhead,
we were summer sledding on the slopes profuse with

pine needles. As I slid down on a garbage can lid holding onto the sides, a stick cut into my right hand from the top, piercing through the palm—a really nasty accident. I ran onto the overhanging porch, where Mother and others were gathered, to show them my bloody fist with the stick still poking through it. As I did so, I began to faint.

Who was there to catch me from falling off the porch? None other than Bob Dabney. But as yet I had not been moonstruck. He was still just like my big brother.

At sixteen Bob got polio—so dreaded in the days before Jonas Salk developed the vaccine. Polio caused Bob to miss a whole year of high school. I was impressed by the courageous decision he made to refuse the iron lung to assist his breathing and later his determination to exercise in order to regain muscle strength. Nolan, ever his buddy, swam with him regularly between the piers in Santa Monica.

All of us were naturals at riding waves and every kind of beach activity—but Bob even more so. He couldn't get enough of the ocean and dreamed of adventures like going to the South Seas, sailing, boating, and studying the stars for navigation. He was born for adventure.

Speaking of adventure, there was one escapade we forever called the boys' "teenage folly." With another friend named Peter, Bob and Nolan bought a four-door Model T Ford cheaply. For months they had that old car in our driveway, rebuilding it. Huddled over a massive spread of maps, they strategically planned a cross-country trip (sans freeways and GPS). The idea was to drive the spruced-up jalopy to Florida and then work their way to Rio de Janeiro on a freighter. Simple.

Several of us girls joined their greasy preparations. We fixed sandwiches and drinks, ran errands, laughed, joked, and just hung around with them. Finally the day of departure came, and a teary farewell it was—trepidation coupled with excitement. Mom supplied a box of canned goods. We girls had baked cookies and packed food to last. As they drove off, there was no mistaking their mission.

Hand lettering across the back declared boldly, RIO OR BUST!

Not many hours later in Cajon Pass, about eighty miles away, the car got stuck in gear and the engine gave out. They actually pushed the car downhill. They sold it and the food for fifty dollars and hitchhiked to Las Vegas. There they took turns gambling—hopefully to make the money to continue their trip. They slept in the park and collected cans to sell so they could eat.

Finally, with no money, they decided to come home and did so by riding a freight train to Los Angeles. Back at last, they called Mother, and we picked up the dirty, smelly bunch—being sure to open the windows wide. Of course, we lost no time ridiculing them mercilessly for their abysmal failure to reach Rio.

The huge, stone fireplace in our living room on Canon Drive drew family and friends together for hours of animated talk, music, singing, and pranks. The dining room held much the same attraction. After meals our conversations lasted way past the last sip of coffee and encompassed every conceivable subject. Whether the topic was current events, history, books, authors, or politics, each discussion was invariably punctuated by gales of laughter.

Young people liked exchanging ideas with Mother and found it easy to confide in her. She was in her element. She loved people, loved to laugh, and loved penetrating conversation. I really think that period of her life was her happiest. She was the center from which all this vitality and energy emanated.

From a remarkably early age, my mom had been a spirited free thinker—a seeker. She had been raised in her early years as a Roman Catholic. When she was sixteen, she could no longer believe that doctrine yet obediently went to church with her family. But after the Catholic service, she would take the trolley to the Christian Science Church. Hearing of this, the priest demanded that she promise not to go anymore. When she told him she could not make that promise, he excommunicated her—a harsh sentence for one so young and a hard blow to her family.

Ironically, when Mother registered Nolan and me as children with the Christian Science Church, they would not allow her to become a member because of her Catholic upbringing. Although she carried their rejection of her as a sorrow, she faithfully attended for years.

As a small girl in Christian Science, I learned the Lord's Prayer, the Beatitudes, and the Ten Commandments. I clearly recall having to sit in church with everything very quiet. I began to realize that I really did not understand what was being read. The older people, however, seemed all-knowing, nodding often in agreement. All this served to heighten the feelings of inadequacy with which I struggled.

Chiseled on the wall of any Christian Science church I ever attended was this quote of Jesus's words from the Bible, found in John 8:32, "Ye shall know the truth, and the truth shall make you free." I guess I stared at it so much that the concept began to draw me. I wasn't quite sure what it meant from a spiritual standpoint, but freedom was certainly attractive.

When we were a little older, Mother became interested in Ernest Holmes's Science of Mind at the Institute of Religious Science. We all went with her regularly to the Science of Mind services held at the Wiltern Theater on Wilshire Boulevard.

Unlike Christian Science, Science of Mind allows medical treatment, viewing the science of medicine as a God-endowed work to benefit mankind. I found Science of Mind more stimulating than Christian Science; however, as a young adult I did not continue to attend the services. When Mother died, Ernest Holmes himself officiated at her memorial. It was most unusual for him to do that personally.

Christianity was a study Mother avidly pursued, along with that of other great religions. She was drawn to Christianity, with its teachings of peace, joy, and love. I do so wish that I had known then what I know now or that she had experienced a mentor like the one God later sent into my life. I can visualize our intense discussions, searching together the wisdom of God's Word.

Dad, on the other hand, was a Unitarian but rarely discussed religion. However, his father, Benjamin Franklin Frizzelle, who incidentally bore an uncanny resemblance to the tall and thin Abraham Lincoln, had been a staunch Bible student and, in fact, sold Bibles. Dad recalled that his large family had gathered in the evenings while his father read to them, page by page, through the entire Bible. Not only did he explain and teach them the Word, but at the same time he used it to teach them to read—a common practice in the days before extensive schoolbooks.

Today that same Bible is at my bedside, a treasure indeed. On the pages provided inside are the dates of our family's births, marriages, and deaths, meticulously handwritten by Grandfather Frizzelle. I have continued that record to the present.

Chapter 3

World War II
Balboa

Our Country Shaken

𝒜 tone of foreboding soon crept into our fireside discussions as they began to focus more and more upon the menacing events unfolding in Europe. The radio went nonstop, informing us of madman Adolf Hitler's ruthless military sweeps over one European nation after another, the relentless bombings of Great Britain, the courage of the English, and Churchill's negotiations with President Franklin D. Roosevelt—two dynamic leaders. The United States helped wherever we could but refrained from direct involvement. Every detail held intense fascination for Bob. Theories were bantered back and forth about the role America might play in Europe and what might precipitate our entry into the conflict.

Bob and Nolan could see the handwriting on the wall and wanted their mothers to sign permission for them to train for the air force. The legal age to enlist was seventeen with parental permission and twenty-one without. Neither mother would agree. Then came December 7, 1941—a day beyond our wildest nightmare.

> The attack (on Pearl Harbor) came as a profound shock to the American people and led directly to the American entry into World War II in both the Pacific and European theaters. The following day (December 8), the United States declared war on Japan.
>
> —*Wikipedia*

Bob had turned twenty-one on December 2. Without a moment's hesitation, he enlisted in the Marine Corps and headed off to boot camp in San Diego. Very soon he shipped out in the Reconnaissance Raider Battalion of the 1st Division, which landed on Talage, then Guadalcanal in the Solomons.

Nolan, having not yet reached that emancipating age, and because he had entered ROTC in order to obtain commission as an officer, had to obey our mother. He left for Stanford without his buddy.

There was a mindset that propelled Bob and that aroused the patriotism of our country at that time. I, as well as the rest of us, saw Bob's action as a personal example of American commitment to everything our country stood for—our inalienable rights of freedom and protection under our great Constitution.

As children in school we pledged allegiance to the flag of the United States of America. We stood together under our flag and sang songs of patriotism—confident we lived under the protection of God and country. The Bible was ever-present in the classrooms. The bonds of faith and patriotism united us. We were ready to give our all to preserve our laws and rights and justice for every citizen.

So when our military was suddenly attacked by the Japanese, as a nation we were stunned yet united behind our president, joining him to protect our country—our country that was founded by determined people seeking religious and political freedom. We were and wanted to remain a free people. We rallied to do whatever each of us could to contribute. We truly rose to the occasion. It meant hardship and unselfish giving of ourselves for the good of all.

Friends and families were suddenly scattered. Women became workers in industries to replace their men. We were united in our fight for freedom and ultimate victory. With stirring songs and warm handshakes of trust, true brotherly love was evident and strong. The entire nation was in action, including one Bob Dabney. I was proud that he was my friend.

At that time I had no inkling of the plans that God was setting in place for me. In his Word we read, "For I know the thoughts that I think toward you, says the Lord, thoughts of peace and not of evil, to give you a future and a hope" (Jeremiah 29:11).

Having graduated from Marlborough in June 1941, I was attending the University of California at Berkeley. I joined the Kappa Alpha Theta sorority and lived in the Theta

House on the Berkeley hillside. But these were college times like none other. Our lives were engrossed in the news and fear of possible Japanese submarine attacks on the West Coast. Blackouts were ordered at night—an eerie experience. From the Theta House we marveled at the sight of all San Francisco shutting off its lights, which gave the dramatic illusion of a giant blanket being spread over the entire city. Our own windows were covered by tightly drawn, black curtains.

It was significant that one of the requirements of my initiation into the sorority was to memorize 1 Corinthians, chapter 13, which is all about the love of God and is a perfect outline of how to love our fellow man. When the dangers of the times invaded my sleep, I took comfort in knowing God's love for me.

One night I had a vivid dream. The backdrop was the threat of the Japanese to our West Coast. The setting was a palatial home with a huge porch. Everyone was frantically dashing here and there. I was on the porch in the midst of the confusion when a shaft of light came down from heaven. An angel on each side of me guided me by the hand up, up, up in the beam of light safely to heaven. I can still see it. The dream's imagery sustained me at that time and even at times later in life when fear was real and personal.

> *God, I know that you give your angels charge over us.*

Those two years in the college atmosphere made me feel more than ever that Bob was showing his maturity and patriotism by going off to fight for our beloved country. By comparison, other boys seemed shallow to me. I wrote to him almost daily, and he wrote to me whenever possible. He later told me my letters were a saving grace to him, for the battles he fought in were horrendous. Our writing drew us so close that we found ourselves able to express our innermost thoughts and dreams, as well as our dreads. We became best friends.

A slogan at the time, "Loose lips sink ships," helped everyone to remember to be cautious with the content of their letters. The troops' letters were run through censors. Additionally, a high-tech method, for that time, was gradually introduced. The system was called V-mail and worked between the United States and either of the two fronts, European or Pacific. It was designed to hinder espionage and save greatly on shipping space.

> V-mail correspondence was on small letter sheets, 17.8 cm by 23.2 cm (7 by 9 1/8 in.) that would go through censors before being photographed and transported as thumbnail-sized images in negative microfilm. Upon arrival to their destination, the negatives would be blown up to 60% of their original size 10.7 cm by 13.2 cm (4 ¼ in. by 5 3/16 in.) and printed.

> According to the National Postal Museum, "V-mail ensured that thousands of tons of shipping space could be reserved for war materials. The 37 mail bags required to carry 150,000 one-page letters could be replaced by a single mail sack. The weight of that same amount of mail was reduced dramatically from 2,575 pounds to a mere

45." This saved considerable weight and bulk in a time in which both were hard to manage in a combat zone.

In addition to postal censorship, V-mail also deterred espionage communications by foiling the use of invisible ink, microdots, and micro printing, none of which would be reproduced in a photocopy.

—Wikipedia

Slow to catch on at first, V-mail was soon embraced by the public and was a real morale booster.

With Nolan and me away at college, Mother was living alone in our Beverly Hills house. She grew concerned about our being separated and asked us to return and finish at the University of California, Los Angeles (UCLA). We agreed. It happened that he and I both got on the same Santa Fe train going south to Los Angeles on the same night—a good thing as Mother had a long drive to pick us up. When we got off in Burbank, she met us, completely unnerved. She had driven all the way from Beverly Hills in complete blackness. We did the same going back home, without even the moon to light the way.

Nolan and I transferred to UCLA and lived at home. In his Spanish class, Nolan met his wife-to-be, Mary Lewis Scales. They were in love, and the rest of us were delighted, as she had won our hearts too. But his service loomed ahead, so no plans for marriage were in place yet.

With the war revving up, there were many calls for volunteer jobs. Besides the USO (United Service Organizations), my friends and I decided to answer the Red Cross's call for junior nurses' aides. We nicknamed ourselves The Bedpan Brigade.

One day I was on duty in the huge, crowded veterans' ward at the LA County Hospital. It was after visiting hours when a vet way down the line of beds called out to me to bring him a vase. I assumed, since it was after visits, that he meant a vase for his flowers. I called back, "I'd be glad to. How large is your bouquet?"

Well, the whole ward howled. Given my *naïveté* and inexperience, how was I to know he meant a urinal? Red with embarrassment, I had to march my way from one end of the ward to the other, clutching the requested "vase." The Bedpan Brigade took on greater meaning.

Seriously, that Red Cross training went far beyond urinals, for we gained experience that exceeded our years. One vital point for me was that I became skilled at giving injections. This would help me later during Mother's illness with cancer.

Meanwhile, Bob was in the thick of action in the Pacific, and I would later learn he had been in the Battle of Guadalcanal.

After six months of hard combat in and around Guadalcanal and dealing with jungle diseases that took a heavy toll of troops on both sides, Allied forces managed to halt the Japanese advance and dissuade them from contesting the control of the island by finally driving the last of the Japanese troops into the sea on 15 January

1943. American authorities declared Guadalcanal secure on 9 February 1943.

—*Wikipedia*

He survived Guadalcanal but had contracted malaria. The good side of that was he was sent stateside on a troop ship to Long Beach for treatment. As soon he could, he called me excitedly for a date. We went to dinner and a movie at the Beverly Hills Theater. When he held my hand, an electric shock went through me. Then he took me home and kissed me good night passionately.

I shut the front door, leaned against it inside, and gasped, "I never thought I'd marry Bob Dabney!" We loved each other more than either of us could believe.

He was stationed at the Long Beach Naval Hospital for his recovery. The malaria brought on fever and chills often, but those attacks were becoming less frequent with medication. Atabrine, the treatment for malaria then, gave his skin a greenish pallor, which we kidded blended with his Marine Corps greens. Nothing was too sacred for our humor. Laughter helped us deal with the gravity. We were just grateful he was alive.

To do my part for the war effort and, I candidly admit, partly to impress Bob, I had gotten a job as a riveter at Douglas Aircraft in Santa Monica—an easy commute from Beverly Hills. My job was working on the wings of C-46 planes. We had to climb onto scaffolding to reach the huge wing as it stood on its brace. There'd be a partner on the opposite side, holding a steel buck bar. I held a two-pound gun with rivets in it and ran the riveter while my partner pushed on the bar so the rivets sealed into the metal. We were real-life versions of the poster girl, Rosie.

> Rosie the Riveter (became) a cultural icon of the United States, representing the American women who worked in factories during World War II, many of whom produced munitions and war supplies. These women sometimes took entirely new jobs replacing the male workers who were in the military. Rosie the Riveter is commonly used as a symbol of feminism and women's economic power.
>
> —*Wikipedia*

Because Bob was at the hospital in Long Beach and I lived in Beverly Hills, getting together wasn't easy. So I put in for a transfer to Douglas Long Beach, and it was granted. I was able to stay with a family friend on Balboa Island. Joan, another very good friend even today, also went to work at Douglas. She was living at her mother's home on Balboa on Ruby Avenue. At 5:30 a.m. each work day I went over to Joan's, fixed some breakfast for us and made sack lunches. Then we met our carpool driver and headed out to work all day, returning about six.

Bob's treatment progressed to the point where he was allowed to leave the hospital daily. He hitched a ride to Balboa, and we filled our hours with fun: swimming, boating, biking, or just walking and talking. One of our places to eat was Jolly Roger's (now Wilma's) known for its hamburgers, which Bob absolutely craved; he had missed them while away. We took the ferry to our other dinner spots, either the Dollhouse or Christian's Hut on the Newport Peninsula.

To encourage my willing reminiscences of Balboa, I have this little painting of our famous ferry. That ferry is still the best shortcut between Balboa and the Newport Peninsula.

Artist, Steve Simon, printed with permission

Very often, our dates included friends who had been playmates and schoolmates—all of us now in similar stages of romance. Joan was dating her future husband, John. Both he and Bob loved boating. We sometimes raced little Sabots (sailing dinghies). Lots of crazy fun.

Occasionally Bob's and my conversations became agonizingly serious, for he would confide to me some of the rigors of his time in combat. I felt honored that he opened up in such a way. I could see it was hard for him, but at the same time, I felt he needed to. How glad I was to be the one he trusted.

I learned the background of what had happened on Guadalcanal, where he had fought in the jungle for months before getting malaria. To hear him tell it was heart-stopping. He was always so animated that I felt I was witnessing it firsthand.

Guadalcanal was the first US battle in the Pacific (August 7, 1942, to February 9, 1943). The Japanese had invaded the Solomon Islands with the goal of capturing each island and eventually dominating the entire Pacific. Control of the Solomons was important to us in order to keep the supply and communication routes open between the United States, Australia, and New Zealand. The islands would also be strategic in our plan to neutralize other Japanese strongholds in the Pacific. Bob's mission, along with his fellow Marines, was to invade on foot, secure the islands, and establish an airfield on Guadalcanal.

Because World War I was proclaimed to be "the war to end all wars," our military had been drastically cut down. The truth is that our country simply wasn't prepared for war. The Merchant Marines bringing supplies to our troops were vital to our successes, but some of their rules of operation were so antiquated at the start of the war that our men suffered because of the confusion.

In Guadalcanal, when the ships anchored and before they could complete off-loading adequate supplies, they came under heavy attack from the approaching Japanese fleet. This resulted in our marines being grossly undersupplied with ammunition as well as food. To survive, our men took rice from Japanese troops they captured. They made fires and cooked in their helmets—Spam, K-rations, and Japanese rice. Bananas were thankfully plentiful.

Our marines went in to gain ground so that the Seabees (the Navy's Construction Battalion) could follow. The Seabees would clear off an area and then lay down giant, perforated steel mats, known as Marston Mats. These served as portable landing strips, allowing our planes to bring in supplies and to refuel.

Most of Bob's buddies had been killed on Guadalcanal. He told me that when he experienced seeing men killed right and left he had said to God that if he was spared, he knew it would be because God had a purpose for his life. From then on, Bob lived his life with that conviction. That he turned to God then means a great deal to me now. I take comfort in the assurance that Bob is with the Lord and that I will see him again someday.

While Bob was recovering from malaria, Nolan graduated and would soon be heading to Quantico, Virginia, to receive his commission and his first orders. His active-duty assignment would be in Hawaii. Wanting to take his love, Mary, with him, he invited her to the Coconut Grove, a famous nightclub, where he presented her with an orchid into which he had tucked a beautiful engagement ring. It was delightfully romantic. We were all thrilled at the prospect of their marriage.

Speaking of romance, there was a little spot on La Cienega in Los Angeles that Bob and I liked to frequent on special dates, where a singer with a melting voice often serenaded the room. We loved sitting near his piano in the corner and never tired of dancing to his love songs. His name was Nat King Cole.

Although Bob and I didn't know what the future held, one thing was sure: we also wanted to get married. The formal rite of proposal got skipped over without our even realizing or minding it—superfluous somehow in view of our feelings and commitment.

When Mother was visiting her friend Kate McCann on Balboa Island, we decided to break the news. We took Kate and Mom to dinner at the Village Inn. Bob suggested a toast to Saturday, the 11th of September. Mother was curious. "Just what exactly are we toasting to?"

Bob revealed that we would like to be married on that day, just one week away! There was good reason for the rush: the doctors had finally released him as fit to return to duty, and he had been given a furlough, starting immediately, for two whole weeks. With boundless optimism, our plan was to prepare in the first week, get married, and still have time for a whole week's honeymoon at Lake Arrowhead. Although one week is no time to prepare for a wedding, wartime imposed its unique and urgent timeframe on every aspect of life.

He raised his glass to Mom and said, "I can't promise Sue wealth, but what I can promise her is an exciting life." That was all Mother needed to hear. She had missed that so with Dad.

The news of our engagement was met with explosions of glee by all. Bob was careful to ask Dad too. Dad showed his pleasure in our news and how much he cared by composing a song for me. My mind easily recalls the lilting melody. Here are the lyrics:

> *Keep those stars shining in your eyes*
> *They will lead me to paradise*
> *There's no other light for me to see*
> *Than the stars shining in your eyes.*

Preparations for the wedding went remarkably smoothly. Mother got the word out, and everyone shifted into high gear. We chose simple gold bands. A traditional wedding veil from the Dabney family was quickly restored for me to wear. Mary and I had a grand time going to Bullock's Wilshire to find my perfect dress and her lovely attendant's dress. That we would soon be sisters-in-law just heightened our excitement. I was overjoyed that we also found a gorgeous dress for her wedding, set for December 22.

We realized the traditional things associated with a wedding—silver, engraved invitations, fancy reception, and so forth—were impossible but quite dispensable. And many friends were too far away—scattered all over the world in wartime service. Invitations to all who could attend were communicated by phone.

Our ceremony was at All Saints Episcopal Church in Beverly Hills on September 11, 1943. Mary and Nolan were our attendants; Bob's little cousin, Patricia Badham (Tishie to us) was our angelic flower girl.

Signing our official marriage certificate that afternoon was a true rite of passage for me. Until then I had felt the weight of my very long name, Suzzanne Frizzelle. I took great delight in changing my first name then and there to Sue and then proudly having Bob's nice short name added to round it off. The name Dabney had been changed from the original French name of D'Aubigné.

Since my family home was being leased at that time to movie star Paul Lucas, we simply greeted guests at the church. Later Mary and Nolan met us in Santa Monica for a celebration dinner. In short—awesome day!

With the war raging in the Pacific, the influx of servicemen and families to the West Coast made it almost impossible to find a hotel room or even a rental. Mother had contacted Uncle Ed to see if he could get a room for us for the night. He was then a colonel in the Air Force stationed in Stockton and a friend of Hernando Courtright, manager of the Beverly Wilshire Hotel.

A few pulled strings later, we were luxuriating in Maxie Rosenbloom's grandly decorated suite, which happened to be vacant at the time. There was even a small kitchen, making it a real hideaway.

The next day, we were off for a memorable week in Arrowhead Village, the drive made possible by friends, who chipped in gas-rationing coupons, and by Mom, who kindly lent us her car.

From Lake Arrowhead we returned to Balboa Island, where I had miraculously found half of a typical beach bungalow for rent at 210 Ruby Avenue. It was painted a lovely yellow with white trim. We felt fortunate to find a place at all. And the rent was right—twenty-five dollars per month.

Our half had a small living room leading into a tiny bedroom, then the kitchen and, beyond it, a miniscule bathroom. But no bath—that was on the landlady's side. Being a beach house, the shower was outside, set over boards on sand. It had a pull chain and ran only cold water. No matter. This was ours for now, and to us it was perfect.

Today our little honeymoon bungalow is officially designated as one of the island's historical homes and still boasts a coat of pretty yellow, trimmed with white. Thanks to such actions by preservationists, some hints remain of what our Balboa was like for me as a child, as well as for Bob and me throughout our lives. Even when we were away in far-flung places, memories of Balboa called us back to that special part of California.

That was quite a season of excitement for Mom and Dad, as quickly following on the heels of our wedding was Nolan and Mary's. The picture below, taken at their reception, can't do justice to the love and pride that were spilling over from the hearts of Mom and Dad as they stood on either side of the handsome, regal couple.

Soon I got a different job soldering wires in airplane plugs at a small feeder plant in Corona del Mar. We didn't have a car, so I carpooled with friends on the island. Bob was transferred to Camp Pendleton. He was making $90 a month before we married and $120 afterward.

We were totally in love, and life was beautiful.

Five months later, at two one morning, a marine buddy knocked on our bungalow door to announce that he would be back in four hours to take Bob and others to report to the base. That was unusual and no doubt signaled action. I braced myself. It turned out that Bob had been assigned to the 5th Marine Division and was scheduled to ship out—destination unknown.

Without Bob, the tiny yellow cottage was cavernous and empty. I was on uncharted water. My world was rocked with the reality of wartime. I felt starkly alone.

Although he was initially training right across from Balboa on Catalina Island, Bob might as well have been far away. From then through the duration of his service in World War II, I would never know for sure where he was.

But the strength of our love sustained me. I knew together we would make it. What a blessing it was for us both that God had joined us in marriage. How important that was for us during that horrid war. It would be one and a half years before I would see Bob again.

With both her children now married and no longer living at home, Mother had decided to pursue a life-long dream of her own—to live in New York City. She leased our home on Canon Drive and found a fabulous apartment at Number 1 Park Avenue. She took to that city just as expected, immediately making friends with a group of wonderful people. To my surprise, she presented me with a most tempting and intriguing invitation—to join her in New York. I hadn't known that she had been considering the inevitability of Bob's being reassigned overseas and had hoped that I would join her there while he was away.

I gratefully accepted her offer; however, just days later I learned that I was pregnant. Instead of going to join her, I asked her if she could come back to live at home again in Beverly Hills. Without hesitation, she set the wheels in motion to return to the West Coast. Over the summer months, I lived with Grandma Nolan and Auntie Margaret in Hollywood until the Beverly Hills house was free.

When Mom returned, I was already far along in my pregnancy. Her presence by my side was a great comfort with Bob gone. Together we settled back into 713 Canon Drive to prepare for the greatly anticipated arrival.

While Bob and I relied on our letters to make our separation bearable, trying to pick a name for our baby became impossible by mail. In the event it was a boy, I wrote to Uncle Ed to ask if I might name the baby after him, Edward James. By that time, Ed was in the European theater and, little did we know, would later be engaged in the Battle of the Bulge. When he responded, it was by telegram.

Mother was visibly shaken when a telegram arrived for me, anxiously fearing that it might be bad news about Bob. She gave it to me nervously, hands trembling. Actually I didn't share Mom's dread of telegrams for I was sure Bob would return safely. I was so happy to be having our baby and so young that I was just thrilled to get a telegram. Uncle Ed simply said, "I would be honored. Congratulations." Wartime required brief cables.

The actual delivery, on January 4, 1945, was emotionally difficult for Mom, particularly since my labor was terrible and long. I was at Good Samaritan Hospital in Los Angeles, where I had been born, and even had the same obstetrician, Dr. Vruwink. He thought it best I stay in the hospital for a full week after the delivery.

The baby's name was still undecided when I held my infant daughter in my arms for the first time, so I'll never forget how remarkable it was that instantly her perfect name came to me—Nina Marie. But I realized Mother might have reservations, since Nina Marie was the name of her first baby daughter, who was stillborn. Right away I asked Mom if giving the baby the same name was okay with her. I was hopeful when she said she'd have to think about it overnight. The next morning, she walked into my room all smiles, saying nothing would please her more. From then on, the baby was not just mine but Mother's too.

Still, the toll of the war was a specter over all of us. It wrought merciless sorrow in families on every side. In spite of all that, Mom and I thoroughly enjoyed our Nina together for the nine more months before Bob returned.

Since I knew full well that there could be nothing specific in Bob's letters regarding his military action, scouring the newspapers for the 5th Marine Division was the only way I could get a vague idea of his whereabouts. Sometimes my heart leapt as I read of the 5th's enemy encounters.

> The 5th Marine Division was a United States Marine Corps infantry division. Created during World War II, the 5th Division saw its first combat action during the Battle of Iwo Jima in 1945 where it sustained the highest number of casualties of the three Marine divisions of the V Amphibious Corps (invasion force). The 5th Division was to be part of the planned invasion of the Japan homeland before Japan surrendered. The 5th Division received the Presidential Unit Citation for extraordinary heroism on Iwo Jima in February 1945 (awarded to the V Amphibious Corps).
>
> —*Wikipedia*

Yet throughout the year and a half Bob was away, I essentially maintained a peace that I can only call divine. I was steady in my belief that he would be back with us, safe and sound. Indeed, he did return safely, but only after fighting in the horrendous battle of Iwo Jima.

Finally, at long last, the war was over—victory had been won. Our men came home!

We rejoiced and couldn't stop giving thanks for the blessings of their survival. Bob immediately bonded with his baby Nina. He could hardly stop playing with her. He was a capable, sweet daddy and thoroughly glad to be alive. Nolan returned as well, as did many dear, mutual friends. Our happiness in having all of our gang together again was indescribable.

Rentals were still hard to come by. Since Mother had the four-bedroom, three-bath, spacious house, she welcomed us all to stay. "Us" included not only Bob, Nina, and me, but also Nolan, Mary, their baby, Roger, and our good friends, Ted and Jean Ptak.

With the men all back and uninjured, it was a continuous house party. Mother reveled in the youthful merriment and joined right in, reserving only the rights to her own big bedroom and sitting room. We teased Mom about her embarrassment at the quantity of empty bottles in the trashcans in the alley behind the house; after all, this was "proper" Beverly Hills.

After news of the Japanese acceptance [of the terms of surrender] and before Truman's announcement, Americans began celebrating "as if joy had been rationed and saved up for the three years, eight months and seven days since Sunday, Dec. 7, 1941", as Life magazine later reported.

—*Time magazine, "Victory Celebrations,"*
8/27/45, Wikipedia

Certainly we all did our part to let out our joy, which had, indeed, been severely rationed.

Thinking back, I believe it was most fortunate that we had that time at Mother's house with others who had also served. Being among their close friends, the fellows were more apt to face the stark images each carried in their heads. Left alone with their wives, whom they would have perhaps wanted to shield, the men might have bottled up those haunting images and allowed them to fester into serious mental battles, possibly crippling their future lives.

Because Bob and I had built such trust through our faithful letters, we were especially blessed to be able to look reality in the face. Nevertheless, it was heart-stopping to hear the details that could not be divulged by letter. The Guadalcanal stories had been harsh enough, but now we heard more, including firsthand reports of the atom bomb.

I had no idea that Bob had been on a ship coming back to the States after Iwo Jima was secured when the atomic bomb changed everything for him. The ship received orders to turn around; there was more duty ahead for the marines on board. Bob was among those redeployed to secure Sasebo and bring order there after the devastation of the war. It was absolutely more dreadful than he could express; I could read it in his eyes and hear it in the tone of his voice. Pure horror.

As good and as healthy as our group time together was, the men had to get themselves reintegrated into civilian life. Nolan, Mary, and baby Roger moved to a new, small house on Veteran in Trousdale Estates, off Pico Boulevard; Nolan followed in Dad's footsteps and pursued optometry. The Ptaks found an apartment.

We stayed on with Mother, while Bob studied real estate. His plan was to join his father in his realty business on Beverly Boulevard. And—gift of gifts—Mom cared for Nina while Bob and I went to Catalina Island for a second honeymoon and started our second baby, Nancy.

Not long afterward, while I was pregnant with Nancy, Mother was stricken with intense abdominal pain. She didn't have a doctor, so I called an ambulance. She was rushed to Good Samaritan Hospital. A cancerous ovarian tumor had ruptured; peritonitis had set in. The cancer spread throughout her body.

She insisted the doctor not tell any of us she had cancer, so we all had to pretend we didn't know the truth. It was unbelievably sad not to be able to express our honest feelings with her. At that time cancer was a shameful thing; a great deal of misunderstanding and misinformation surrounded it. For nine months at home, she slowly succumbed to the rampage within her.

When Nancy was born June 30, 1947, Mother visibly rejoiced. She wanted to see the baby as much as possible and loved me to nurse Nancy in her room. Thanks to Dad, Mother was able to have a hospital bed brought into her sitting room as well as have a night and a day nurse in attendance.

For some reason, Mom liked how I gave shots and insisted that I be the one to administer them, rather than the nurses. Here is where that Red Cross training I had received proved invaluable, for toward the end, I was administering morphine to her every two hours at night. As cheerfully as possible, I did what I could to make her comfortable, all the while keeping up the façade of silence concerning the real issue facing us.

A Christian Science practitioner worked with her every two weeks. The important thing to Mom was the spiritual strength and comfort that she gained by prayerfully repeating her favorite Bible quotes, including 1 John 3:1 and the Christian Science Scientific Statement of Being.

As a gentle aside, remember Art, her ardent suitor? He was now a widower and still a good friend. They dated for a short time, until her illness rendered her too weak. It was a sweet, happy time for them both. Truth be told, he had been her first true love and she, his.

Then Mother was gone. Nancy was only six weeks old at the time, and over the years it has been uncanny to me to see so much of Mom reflected in her.

Mom had had a way of saying with acceptance when events brought changes, "That door is closing." But to me it seemed that she had now found a wide-open, welcoming door. I sensed that she had glided through it in a way that left her presence with me, for I do feel she has never left me. I like to think there is a silver thread that connects me to her, a symbol of the deep love we shared. And I believe that same thread exists with my daughters, connecting us all eternally. It's a comforting thought to me.

Mom's funeral was held at Forest Lawn, where her dear brother, Edward James Nolan, is buried.

Chapter 4

West Los Angeles
Corona del Mar
Saipan
Washington, DC

The Intrigue Begins

*A*fter Mother's death, Nolan and I sold our family home
of fifteen years in Beverly Hills. The selling price will
put the times into perspective: it was $27,000. Bob and I were
able to buy a brand-new house near Nolan and Mary's on
Veteran Avenue in Trousdale Estates.

As a returning veteran, Bob could take advantage of the
government's GI Bill for educational assistance. He eagerly
took the chance to learn to fly his own small plane and
enrolled in flying classes at the airfield in Santa Monica—
still there, by the way. He and two classmates invested in a

Cessna 120, a single-engine, two-seater with a compass and radio (only).

He quickly became adept and flew often. One Saturday he excitedly suggested that he and I fly to the Del Mar horse races. So off we went, enjoying the sunny day and views, in spite of my shivering with apprehension by his side. Soon I could take a full breath—we landed safely at the Del Mar field near the track.

We were having great fun choosing the winning horses, when all of a sudden, as often happens in the coastal areas, a huge blanket of fog rolled in. We could hardly make out the horses. We turned to each other and exclaimed in unison: "Let's get out of here—fast!"

I must admit Bob amazed me. Steadily he took off into the fog. We flew up into and out of the thick haze and headed due north. There was a stretch of tense silence, broken only by the hum of the engine. Then we spotted the airfield. Landing safely, each of us let out a loud exhale of relief and promptly burst out laughing as we climbed down to the tarmac.

Several months later, Bob sold his interest in the Cessna to one of his friends. Sadly we learned shortly thereafter that the new owner had crashed in the Santa Monica Mountains, killing himself and demolishing the plane.

Bob struggled a while at real estate and then changed direction, getting a job with Bill White at the customhouse brokerage firm of Frank P. Dow. He quickly became assistant manager and was well on his way to becoming established. Meanwhile, Nolan had returned to college to get his doctorate in optometry at the University of Southern California (USC) to be able to take over Dad's business.

Living near Nolan and Mary, with many good friends in common who also had children, made for wonderful companionship over the next couple of years. We young parents were like kids ourselves, so our get-togethers were usually boisterous and wild, with many happy shenanigans. And it was a time when our little ones, cousins and friends alike, began lifelong friendships.

Then all too soon, another war broke out. Korea this time.

> The Korean War (25 June 1950–27 July 1953) was a war between the Republic of Korea and the Democratic People's Republic of Korea. It was primarily the result of the political division of Korea [with the 38th Parallel being the line of separation] by an agreement of the victorious Allies at the conclusion of the Pacific War at the end of World War II. The United States of America provided 88% of the 341,000 international soldiers which aided South Korean forces in repelling the invasion, with twenty other countries of the United Nations offering assistance. It was the first significant armed conflict of the Cold War.
>
> —*Wikipedia*

Bob had often said to me that if the country ever needed him again, he would return to active duty. I knew how deep his conviction was, and I had agreed. But that had been some time ago, and things were different now, I reasoned. After all, we had two little girls. I said some of this out loud, but for the most part the struggle was with myself. It came down to this: would I be true to my word to him or not? But my inner dialogue had taken too long. Before I could formulate a proper counter-proposal or give a speech of consent, Bob was back with the Marine Corps at Camp Pendleton. By default, I was on board.

The girls and I traipsed behind and found a small rental home in Corona del Mar. Our pretty first house was sold for $13,000. Incidentally, those houses in Trousdale Estates were later confiscated to make way for the 405 Freeway.

We adjusted to our sudden transplant from Westwood to Corona del Mar, and actually liked the area very much. It was terrific being nearer the beach with the kids, and soon new friends were woven into the fabric of our lives.

This small painting of Corona del Mar Beach resides with me and gives me great pleasure, as it reflects that time perfectly.

Artist, Steve Simon, printed with permission

Another unexpected jolt came in 1953 while at Camp Pendleton. Bob was recruited by the CIA. Our first assignment would be on the tiny island of Saipan, way out in the vast Pacific.

Returning to the Marine Corps for Korea was one thing, but the prospect of living a possibly dangerous life undercover, exposing my two girls to untold threats and who knew what else—well, quite another thing!

This time I was verbose with my protests, doing my utmost to convince Bob that he had already given more than enough for our country. He had fought in the harsh, hand-to-hand battles of Guadalcanal (1943) and Iwo Jima (1945), and then served during the rehabilitation of Japan. Not to mention that he had, again, voluntarily joined the Marine Corps for the Korean conflict. Surely this decision to enter the CIA was over the top.

After much discussion and private soul-searching, I made a resolute decision that we would always, even beyond the CIA service, be bonded together as a loving, happy family—come what may. Believe me, that stand would be put to many tests, but the bottom line was unity in love. God was building character in me.

So Bob went off to Washington, DC, for training, and my job was to prepare our household and our family for the move to Saipan. You can imagine how many times I had to repeat to myself the commitment to follow Bob. Remember his promise of adventure to Mom when we announced our intended marriage? She was probably smiling down on us.

Belongings had to be sorted into essential-and-take or non-essential-and-store. Of course, the girls and I had to get many inoculations (tetanus, typhoid, diphtheria, typhus, and smallpox). Those vaccinations made the fact that we were actually leaving the country very real, especially when the girls had some adverse reactions to them.

Bob returned briefly from DC to see us on the West Coast before heading for Saipan, where we would later join him.

The wars had inspired the development of commercial planes, but they were in limited use; most long distance travel was still by automobile, bus, train, or ocean liner. The US government had contracted with Boeing for employee transportation, and so our flight would be on Pan Am's Boeing 377 Stratocruiser. Their one flight a day from Los Angeles to Hawaii (not yet a state) was the only way to fly across the Pacific. The Stratocruiser was impressive in size with its two stories, especially when seen from ground level.

With my eyes still wet from teary farewells with family and friends, I approached the towering stairway to the airplane with determination, while clutching a hand of each daughter, six and eight years old, with a firm grip. Memory replays that walk across the carpeted tarmac in slow motion. We were being blown mercilessly by the winds, which seem to claim runways everywhere as their exclusive territory, intensified by the whirling propellers.

I felt like a big, reluctant, balking bull being dragged along by a rope—or was it something else? Out of fear, I began to laugh on purpose. It was contagious. I really believe that laughter is every mother's merciful trick. By the time we reached the gaping door of our "spaceship," we were ready for we knew not what.

In truth, Bob's mission was quite spooky to me. When the three of us entered our little compartment designed for four passengers, behold, there sat the fourth—a small, quiet Chinese man with a Fu Manchu beard and beady eyes. Naturally I was sure he was a spy. He said not a word but simply watched our every move. Lightly, yet nervously, I joined in chatter with the children while keeping my eye on him. Our undercover life had begun.

Our flight to Honolulu lasted eight bumpy hours as our cruising altitude was only twenty thousand feet. On our arrival, Nancy tumbled down the departure stairs and had to be bandaged up at the first-aid station. After a lay-over, the flight on to Guam was much smoother, although longer by four hours. And—exhale—Fu Manchu was no longer with us.

What an adventure the girls had as we staggered along the narrow aisle, exploring the aircraft. It doesn't seem possible now, but the pilot actually invited us into the cockpit and showed us the controls.

Individual staterooms off the walkway were equipped with bunks, padded bench seats, and a small bathroom. Our bunks were prepared for us, and our meals politely served. We had no complaints, and there was no boredom. Besides, we had rehearsals to do for our snappy song-and-dance routine of "Side by Side" that we had planned for Daddy. The girls enjoyed practicing it, because we *were* traveling along and singing our song.

Don't know what's comin' tomorrow
Maybe it's trouble and sorrow
But we'll travel the road,
Sharin' our load, side by side.

Through all kinds of weather
What if the sky should fall?
As long as we're together,
It doesn't matter at all!

Any uncertainty I might have had during the trip was well worth it when we landed in Guam. There to greet us was Bob—handsome in his tropical tan and Bermuda shorts—smiling broadly, arms wide, and very glad to hug his girls at last.

We were whisked by van to the company house, where we would stay overnight. It was a large tropical grass hut on stilts, with a typical thatched roof. The lower level was open, sensibly, for rain flow, pigs, chickens, etc. Stairs took us up to the living quarters, which were complete with rattan furniture, grass rugs, and mosquito nets hanging over the beds.

It was indescribable joy to be together again. The girls chatted on and on. We all did, relating every detail of what had happened over our weeks apart. We hugged and laughed, finally pausing for a briefing about what our new life would be like for the next two years. Underlying the exhilaration was the unspoken conviction that whatever lay ahead, we could tackle it—as long as we were together.

The next day we boarded a covert company plane to Saipan, an island in the Marianas closer to Japan. It was unnerving to be in the much smaller, unmarked plane, but with the presence of Bob and the kindness of the pilot and copilot, we soon relaxed. After the one-hour flight north, what a thrill it was to approach our island destination below! It was lush and green, set like an emerald in the very deep blue ocean.

A score of people with bundles of colorful, fragrant leis waited to welcome us on the little airstrip. Before long, they would be friends who could be counted on like family.

In no time, we were aboard a caravan of weapons carriers and jeeps, weaving our way through narrow asphalt and coral streets to our compound. We saw no stores or houses except in the one native village of Garapan. The most noticeable structure there was a lovely gray and white Catholic church.

The executive director who was showing us around gave us a recap of Saipan's recent history. Nine years earlier, during World War II, the island had been bitterly fought over by the 2nd and 4th Marines and the Japanese forces who occupied it. It had been a terrible battle, which had left the island largely abandoned.

Unfortunately, during the war, the Japanese had been propagandized to believe the Americans were barbaric. Rather than face the imagined horrors of being captured by the barbarians, many of them committed suicide by jumping off Marpi Point to the rocks, sharks, and violent surf below. Even when we arrived nine years later, the island still had a very small population.

We learned our own little community consisted of about two hundred people living in a cluster of Quonset huts along the beach (mostly duplexes). Each residential unit was twenty by forty-eight feet. Much larger Quonsets housed the movie theater with dirt floor and wooden bench seats, and others housed the clubhouse, administrative offices, storage, and the post office. One of the storage Quonsets contained about 2,000 books abandoned by the US Marine forces that had captured the island from the Japanese in 1944.

I remarked to the director, "What a shame that with so many intelligent people here, there's no library."

He said to me, "The job is yours!"

I smiled. *Fancy me—a librarian!*

The jeep then pulled up to what would be our home for the next two years. Nina and Nancy jumped out, ready and racing to explore. Our Quonset had two bedrooms, a small kitchen, living/dining room, front porch, wash area, and bathroom. The Quonset's simple construction had been transformed by appealing tropical furnishings. Its many screen windows had shutters to be secured in case of sudden rain. We were told that trucks went by every two weeks spraying out DDT to try to minimize mosquitoes. As an added precaution, we soon developed the daily habit of regular squirts of the insect repellant Sketolene all over each of us.

Not much time elapsed before I decided to take the director up on his librarian idea. It was the greatest job for me. At my disposal was a crew of laborers to build the stacks, tables, comfortable chairs, lighting, file cabinets, desk, and card catalog. I spent weeks going over each book, cataloging, carding, and filing. I even issued library cards to each person. It was a joke at first. "Where do you think I'm going?" was the retort, since we were rigidly restricted to our small island.

The library cards turned out to be a help, because I could find a book if it was needed while checked out. The companionship brought about by discussing what we had read fostered great camaraderie. Soon I was given a budget to order new books from the States, using the *New York Times* book review section to pinpoint our selections. We were hungry for more; there was great anticipation for each new shipment.

All supplies and provisions were flown to us from Japan by our pilots, Dutch Brongersma and Bobby Hamblin, in the "blacked-out" Company C-46. They were our heroes, bringing us everything for our little store—in spite of the fact that the supplies themselves had a few drawbacks. It was standard to have powdered milk and eggs. But what took a little more getting used to was finding the flour weevily, the sugar hardened by humidity, and the bread stale. Imagine our delight when some fresh milk or candy bars made it into our shipment! While our clubhouse kitchen was also supplied that way, our creative chef managed to consistently surprise us with specialties like Baked Alaska, local fried frogs' legs, and occasionally even Kobe beef steaks—such a treat.

A rare, very strong typhoon came through while we were there. Our camp was evacuated to a giant Quonset that had been set into the mountainside for maximum safety. The children thought the typhoon adventure was a ball— playtime and sleep-overs with friends. It was exciting and scary at the same time. How the chef did it, we never knew, but he never missed preparing three meals a day for us all. Returning to our little Quonsets on the beach, we found them severely damaged by the fierce winds and rain. Three had been completely washed out to sea, leaving only their cement foundations. Rapid team work by everyone restored our base, and strengthened our appreciation for each other.

We families established a camp Sunday school and church service, though the facilities were rustic, to say the least. All too aware of our circumstances, the adults knew how important this would be to keeping ourselves and our families grounded.

There is no doubt that Mother's influence to have God front and center motivated me to work hard to establish this as an integral part of our lives. Though unaware of the real and personal presence of Jesus, and though I didn't have the whole picture, I was on the right track. I understand now that I did not have to be all cleaned up and good enough for him. What I knew of him was good, and I wanted to share what I knew—that there is more to this life than meets the eye.

At home I was consistent with a practice I had set in place from the time the girls were very little. Every night we would kneel together by their bed to say prayers of thanksgiving and petition. Besides the Lord's Prayer, I taught my children another my mother had taught me: "Father-Mother God, loving me, guard me while I sleep, guide my little feet up to thee. I thank you, dear God, for showing me how happy a little girl can be." The girls' prayers were simple, yet they were the sweet ones of children.

Nina and Nancy told me they remembered our time in Saipan as the very happiest of their childhood. The four of us were able to share time together, for Bob joined us whenever he could. We spent hours exploring the island. War had left remnants of rusted-out tanks and scattered ammunition. There were intriguing caves, dense jungle roads, and gracefully bent tree branches bedecked with flowers.

We splashed along beautiful beaches where we made a game of searching for colorful glass balls. These balls had been used by Japanese fisherman to provide flotation for their fishing nets. To our good fortune, some got loose and floated down with the tides from Japan. Our exotic collection grew. And on an abandoned airstrip, ten-year-old Nina learned to drive our assigned jeep, and Nancy learned to steer by sitting on Bob's lap. They thought it was great fun.

Christmas was unique on our little spot in the Pacific. Any gifts we gave had to be ordered months in advance— from Sears and other catalogs. We mothers pored over the enticing pages, charmed by all that was available so far away. This was our shopping spree! Months later, as things arrived, we carefully marked and surreptitiously hid each item until the big day.

And how was Santa to arrive on this tropical island? By parachuting from an airplane, of course! All thanks to our faithful pilots. On the thrilling day, everyone gathered in great anticipation as first his bundle of toys, and then Santa himself, dropped from the sky to land just out of sight on an open field nearby. To everyone's delight, Santa soon came into view, sitting atop the firetruck, smiling broadly, and waving to greet us all. With his bag full of goodies beside him, he led the parade of excited families to the clubhouse where he ceremoniously distributed gifts. What a thrill for the girls—and satisfying for us as well.

Wanting to keep the children in touch with life in the States, my best friend, Helen, and I asked the other mothers with little girls if there would be any interest in our starting a Brownie troop. And yes, there was. We officially registered with the Girl Scouts of America. Our meetings were regular and serious. We followed the requirements carefully for earning badges.

The most ambitious challenge was an overnight camping trip, hiking down to Tanapag Beach. After setting up simple, surplus canvas pup tents, it was non-stop cooking, eating, storytelling, and singing. That night, there was a torrential downpour. We got completely drenched while scrambling to patch up holes in the tents to keep dry. To top it all, I was six months pregnant. Crawling around inside the tents on my hands and knees, my baby bump and I were the brunt of much teasing and laughter.

Those two years on Saipan, however, were not all fun and games for us. Bob was involved in the training of dedicated men from nearby nations, preparing them to free China from the communist dictator Mao Tse-tung. In a military sweep throughout the huge country of China, Mao had driven our friend, Chiang Kai-shek, out of the mainland and onto Formosa (now known as Taiwan).

> In 1946, civil war broke out in China between the Chinese Nationalist Party (known as the Kuomintang or KMT) and the Communists. In 1949, the Communists were victorious, establishing the People's Republic of China. Chiang Kai-shek and the remaining KMT forces fled to the

island of Taiwan. There Chiang established a government
in exile . . .

—*BBC History*

At that time (1953) mainland China was considered to
be in a "Temporary Communist Rebellion" and there was
hope and support for a reestablishment of a free Republic of
China on the mainland.

Bob, with his knowledge and determination, was
passionate to maintain freedom from the tyranny of
Communism wherever it reared its ugly head. We were
in the grips of the grim, cold, Cold War. There were no
formal battlefields. Government domination held the people
captive, and the people's way of life was at stake.

These were still the relatively early days of the CIA
(established by act of Congress in 1947 to replace the Office of
Strategic Services of World War II). It was a highly respected
and effective agency of the US government. It hired the
finest young men from top universities, from businesses,
and from within our armed forces. Because their work was
covert, the public was generally unaware of their activity.
When it achieved great successes, not many knew, but when
some flop occurred, much was made of it by the uninformed
press. It was a somewhat thankless job, but the agents were
dedicated to their cause.

When I think back on that darker side of our two years
in Saipan, I perceive it as a certain valley-like experience.
We had become intricately entangled in the CIA's web of
conspiracy. By its very nature, the CIA must use deception.

The result was that our whole family was drawn into a false life. Saipan was only the beginning.

As a mother, it took strength beyond my own to be able to adapt to the many restrictions imposed upon us in Saipan and the very different way of raising children. One major hurdle was explaining to our two young ones (to whom Bob and I wanted to impart values—honesty being high on the list) that we would be playing a game of make-believe where no one would be known by their real last names. I am sure it was through God's grace that I managed to impart ethics, and I feel I did it well for we came away stronger and with a huge cache of adventuresome memories to boot.

When Bob's Saipan assignment drew to a close, we felt genuine sadness to be leaving friends, yet it was countered by the pure elation of heading home. After a poignant send-off, we boarded the company plane for Guam and then flew on to Hawaii and the States. By then, I was seven months pregnant. Flying for me in that condition was not advisable, but we strongly desired to have our baby in the States, so off we went.

In spite of what must have been considerable jet lag, we enjoyed a brief but joyous reunion with family in Los Angeles. Then we were airborne again for Washington, DC. It was midsummer heat in 1955, and Debby was fast on her way. Her birth date would be August 22.

With adrenalin stoked by anticipation, we accomplished a formidable to-do list without a day to spare. Besides Bob's getting his new CIA assignment, we bought a car, found a rental home, established my obstetrician at Washington University Hospital, enrolled the girls in school, and handled the endless details that are the hidden mountain under any move.

The house we found to rent was in Alexandria, Virginia. It was a typical two-story, red brick home in a lovely wooded neighborhood, actually called Beverly Hills. At last, household items were retrieved from storage and arranged. Oh, the joy of a washing machine, lots of hot water, a vacuum cleaner, a bathtub, and even running water we could drink from the tap!

Debby arrived on cue. She was a treasure that made our lives positively overflow with joy. She was a perfect gift to Bob and me—there's no other way to explain her. And to Nina and Nancy, it felt like playing dolls all the time.

The girls' new school was only two blocks from the house, so they easily walked the short distance. On cold days I had tea and cookies ready by the glowing fireplace to welcome them before they started homework or playtime with baby Debby. Bob came home regularly after work, and we cherished our private family time together.

We were busy, yes, but such happiness! And this doesn't even take into account the thrill of being back on the terra firma of the good old USA. Though it wasn't the right coast, we were home none the less. There was nothing like living again in our country, which we loved so dearly. My heart beat with gratitude. I often say every American should live at least two years outside this country in order to really appreciate the goodness of it.

For me, that period was one of our happiest—my cup was full. We were safe with our little family, intact and unscathed. For a while, we were living a normal life.

Our respite in Alexandria lasted about two years and then Bob received an assignment to live and work in Bangkok, Thailand, for a two-year period. As it turned out, the bliss of a permanent US home was not to be ours for a long while. During the next two decades, we would be in and out of the country, but our goal remained to return to the States and live in the Newport Beach/Balboa area of Southern California.

Chapter 5

Bangkok

Our Asian Home

So there we were—off to another faraway place with a "strange-sounding name," as the popular song went. It was the summer of 1957. Deb was then nearly two years old—not the perfect time to travel, we found out. Bob and I literally walked her across the Pacific. She had been such a placid little one until the flight, but the altitude put pressure on her tender ears and distressed her terribly. Nina and Nancy were natural little mothers, playing with her, distracting her, and soothing her. They were a tremendous help to us.

We had stop-overs in Hawaii, Japan, and Hong Kong, getting our first taste of the rigors of clearing through customs in huge, bustling airports. I don't think I ever got used to having our carefully packed suitcases rummaged through for all to see. And documents! Each country had its unique system of red tape. Patience turned out to be the best antidote.

And thank God that Bob was the kind of man he was. He could keep an eye on everything. Just as I felt I might lose track of one of the girls in the confusion, he would seemingly read my mind, and I'd see that he had the children and everything else under his radar. He was my comfort and safe place.

Landing at Thailand's Don Muang Airport immediately engaged our senses. Bangkok was known as "the Venice of the Orient" at that time, because transportation and commerce were largely carried out through extensive waterways that ran throughout the city. There was a certain heavy aroma due to the many canals, humidity, and heat. Nevertheless, we were cordially met and efficiently shepherded through the airport's procedures—bringing immediate gratitude into my heart for the Thais. In my associations with the Thai people, I found them to be natural diplomats—friendly, wise, and happy, yet crafty in their own inimitable way.

Many years before, the name of this land had been changed from Siam to Thailand, meaning "land of free," a name with high significance for the people. It has never been conquered by another nation, although the French, English, Japanese, Vietnamese, and Burmese each tried.

In conversations with my dad about our new home, he could never relate to its being called Thailand. To him it would always be Siam. Making matters more amusing, he was known to confuse Siam with Syria. Of course, he knew our laughter at his geography was just loving teasing.

We were driven through the honking traffic of the city to the gorgeously gaudy, very large Erawan Hotel. Immediately, we were transported to another world and time.

The girls whispered excitedly as we examined the gilded walls, plentiful Buddhas, winding staircases, and high ceilings. Everywhere there were lavish flower arrangements and leis. Graceful ladies glided by in their vibrant Thai silk dresses. Even the women servants were adorned in silk.

The courtyard held within its inviting walls a stunning garden, the centerpiece of which was a large, free-form swimming pool rimmed by inviting lounge chairs. Spectacular flowers boasted every hue imaginable and lent their varying scents to the air. Looking more closely, we discovered delicately sculpted plants and breathtaking orchids, climbing unrestrained. Vivid frangipani trees offered cool shade and beauty. A Jacuzzi, relatively new to us at the time, tempted us with new sensations. And a team of elegant waiters, like actors giving life and breath to a stage, provided the most courteous and sensitive service one could imagine. I was enchanted.

The Erawan's stark, modern-day successor, although an elegant five-star hotel, does not in any way convey the unique grandeur that was our experience.

Our roomy suite had two bedrooms and a large bathroom with a bidet, which, of course, fascinated the children. As odd as it might seem, the bidet was soon their favorite spot for sailing little boats. Although in my opinion bidets should be standard in all bathrooms, we refrained from using ours as intended to allow the kids some freedom in their rather restrictive hotel situation.

Bob masterfully took care of travel matters and hotel routines while contacting necessary business associates. He was assigned to the US Embassy, more specifically to USOM (United States Overseas Mission). Thailand had requested help from our country in multiple ways, one of which was to assist the Thai police in securing their vast borders from communist aggressors.

Politically our countries were loyal to each other. That loyalty played out also on a personal level during our time there, largely due to Bob's innate ability to relate so well to people of very different cultures. He developed a genuine passion for the Thais. They shared mutual trust, which enabled Bob to be effective on their behalf. He drew strength from the fact that while he was serving them, he was also serving his country in the process.

From our base at the Erawan, we proceeded to search for an affordable and suitable home, one that would be close to schools, work, and city conveniences. As our agent took us around, owners were curious about us too since Caucasians at the time were a novelty in Thailand. Some would squeeze Debby's chubby white arms affectionately with titters. Many expressed sadness for us, however, woefully shaking their heads because we had three girls and no boys.

Six weeks passed before the perfect house surfaced. It turned out to be a very pretty, two-story, modern, walled compound. It met every requirement, including being close to the center of town and the Erawan Hotel, where much of our activity was centered.

Life within the compound was a complex interaction between us and the servants, who were a must to make it all happen. Their monthly pay was a fifty-kilogram burlap bag of rice, twenty-five dollars, and on-site living quarters. Since the servants lived there, we had no need for a house key—someone was always at home.

It is important to realize, as we had to, that we were living among people whose customs were unfamiliar on every level. The one that affected us immediately was that it is thought rude and disrespectful to hold your head level with or above the head of a more highly ranked person. When Bob and I had our first dinner prepared and served by our new servants, they entered the room on their knees, in deference to what they considered our superior rank. Although we knew it was vital to observe that rule in Thai society, we were in control of our own home, so we asked them not to approach us in that manner and explained to them a little of our American culture.

Regarding household servants, there was an accepted understanding of mutual dependency, meaning that they were treated as an extended part of the family. Their personal needs, beyond their work, were considered. Their service to the home was appreciated as essential; consequently, what could be done to enable them to have a good life and perform their tasks was regarded as a normal exchange. I found that same mindset in the Thai families we came to know. The practices of give and take resonated naturally with us and nurtured strong relationships between us and our servants.

Meanwhile, during our settling-in period, Nancy and Nina were enrolled in the International School Bangkok, which was attended by children of every nationality, except Thai. While the school incorporated American curricula, there were major differences. Even the building itself was a novel experience for them. It was a simple, bare, wooden, two-story structure with squeaky planked hallways and wonderfully open ventilation. The walls were low half-walls, leaving the space above wide open without shutters or screens. The breeze, birds, and lizards came through freely. Regardless–and perhaps because of the differences— the girls were very happy there and did well.

Entering our new life in Bangkok was a serious step further into the clandestine world in which we were now thoroughly enmeshed. Thoughts like "spooky" or "shadowy" at first excited me and my imagination but made me feel uncertain. Thankfully I soon gained reassurance that we were operating under a carefully programmed, safe routine with layers of protection. We were extremely well briefed and prepared for any eventuality. All the help we could possibly need was available to us. We were instructed and encouraged to adhere to the proven protocol in place for government personnel.

An American overseas is actually a responsibility of the ambassador to that country. All citizens are expected to inform him of their presence and the nature of their work in his territory. For that reason I had proper calling cards made that were required to be presented when visiting the ambassador and his wife at their residence or attending other important social events. Those cards were meticulously filed for reference and for consideration of our inclusion in future activities. I came to appreciate the importance of a wife's role; it is a reflection upon her husband's record and has a direct influence on his career.

The impact of our move to Bangkok was a lifestyle change comparable to commoners suddenly becoming royalty. Anyone connected to the embassy was not only exceptionally special to the Thais, but due their utmost respect. Of course, Bob's association with the embassy through USOM was covert, but to the Thais, we were perceived only as United States Embassy personnel, and treated accordingly. I was thrilled to serve in any capacity. I thought of myself, on a very small scale, as a personal ambassador for our country. That thought made me want to behave myself—to show kindness toward and interest in everyone I met.

The fact was that our lives were, of necessity, immersed into the lives and culture of the leaders of Bangkok and Thai society. That being said, there were very many times when I felt an unsettling discomfort. It was as though I wore an invisible mask, particularly at cocktail and dinner parties among people I didn't know. Being not quite the person I appeared to be made for an uncomfortable way to socialize.

Language presented a formidable challenge. While those with whom we socialized spoke English, my ears had to become accustomed to the accents of even their English words in order to grasp the meaning. Their tones when speaking English were filled with the complex lilts of Thai. The Thai language has forty-four consonants, thirty-two vowels, and five tones of pronunciation. Saying the same word in five different tones can communicate five different meanings. In the marketplace communication was simpler, because gestures were commonly accepted and understood.

Through his work, Bob met a unique man by the name of Khun Amorn. "Khun" is an honoring title, appropriate for either a man or a woman; Amorn was his given name.

Men often added a word that sounded like "Krop" to the end of what they were saying as another measure of respect. When Bob addressed him, all three words would roll rapidly, happily into one—"Khunamornkrop!" It was an indication of their fun-loving, mutual friendship.

Khun Amorn introduced us to the Friday Night Friends, a diverse, multinational group of people who met weekly. A delightful woman by the name of Khun Ying hosted this gathering at her home, and we went regularly. She was a strong, exceptionally smart Thai lady whom I grew to know well.

Her home deserves the adjective palatial. It was of the traditional open-air Thai design, drawing in as much of the outdoors as possible. Because of the extremely hot and humid weather in Bangkok, fans of all sizes were everywhere, circulating the air constantly. Servants with handheld wicker fans provided additional relief. No doubt the advent of air-conditioning has altered those customs now.

The Friday Friends shared loyal, lasting relationships. Many had known each other since childhood. A number of the ladies, like Khun Ying and another called Khun Chern, were of royal standing, though very modest about that. Some guests were in the academic field; some, in government; some were social friends; and some, missionaries.

Many of the Friends had gone to Watana School for Girls, and it was the Watana Christian Church that our family attended. What a good thing it was for me when we found it! Until then I had felt parched for shared worship in this culture where little is known of Christ. I have to admit that it was amusing to hear our friends say that they loved Jesus and then giggle and add shyly, "But we love Buddha too!"

Khun Ying had been brought up as a Christian. She and I found plenty of ground on which to build rapport. She possessed a firm dedication to the education of young girls and, in fact, owned and managed the huge Watana girls' school. With native English speakers being in high demand, she asked if I would agree to teach the language there—an invitation I was glad to accept. She made it even more attractive by graciously having her driver pick me up for classes.

Amorn, while a sensitively deep man, was also a comic cutup, reminding us of Yul Brynner in *The King and I*. We all dressed informally for comfort on those Fridays, and Amorn was most casual in his wide, colorful, Arabian-style pants, which he wore with just a plain white T-shirt. He took great pleasure in hijinks, only too happy to emulate Yul, the king. His lean, muscular body and bald head enhanced the impersonation. Jokes flew around the room between us all. It was a great time to unwind and just relax amid a group of caring, interesting, and interested people. Occasionally, captivating Thai dancers would entertain us.

As we sat chatting, servants in the background remained vigilant and responsive to our every wish—anything to make the guests feel comfortable. They moved about, bringing drinks and offering trays with an enticing selection of delicious food. Sometimes a guest, weary or tense, might signal for a gentle foot or shoulder massage, just as we might from a trusted friend. Keep in mind the relationships that existed between Khun Ying and her servants. Observing the hierarchy of privilege did not preclude personal consideration of each other. Kindness was the thread.

Children usually did not come to our Friday nights, but a few times ours were invited. Nancy and Deb like to remember the warm welcome that was extended to them. Even though hugs are not part of the Thai culture, they felt embraced none the less and thoroughly enjoyed the delicious food and entertainment.

Steadily we gained understanding of the subtleties that are so much a part of social interaction in Thailand, where body language is as important as words. Gradually it became second nature for Bob and me to know when and how to do the *wai*—the prayer-like position of the hands in greeting while simultaneously bowing to the right degree, depending upon the person's status. That knowledge was important as our social commitments increased.

During our time there, several relatives of our Thai business associates and our Friday Friends passed away, and Bob and I were greatly honored to be invited to their traditional ceremonies. We learned their ways of respecting the dead, particularly if the deceased had been a prominent or wealthy individual. The body was kept on display in a room set aside in their home for that purpose. The length of time before cremation could last anywhere from one month to as long as an entire year. The room would be blanketed with exquisite flower arrangements and a great deal of burning incense. Lights and decorations were elaborate, often including a large portrait of the person. Also a portrait of the king and/or queen would be prominently displayed. The body lay in an open casket for a week, when the first and most significant memorial service took place. After that, the casket was closed.

The family sent engraved invitations to distinguished guests, relatives, and friends. These memorial gatherings were at appointed intervals, such as the seventh, fiftieth, and hundredth days after the death. The extended time of the rituals demonstrated love and respect for the deceased and were thought to benefit the departed before their spirit was released through cremation.

The women wore black, and the gentlemen wore white with black armbands. Shoes, as usual, were left at the door—a pleasure really, as the wooden floors were immaculately polished, pleasing to the touch. Monks were present, adding a great deal of dignity to the affair. Each guest had the opportunity to bow and pay homage to the person by lighting a joss stick of incense and placing it by the body.

All was not solemn, however. After the Buddhist rituals were complete for that evening, the guests would retire to another part of the house to celebrate and appreciate the life of the deceased. There were always musicians present, often joined by elegantly attired dancers who performed the traditional dance called the Ramwong. The guests were expected to dance a far less demanding, folk-style version of the dance. While our stiff American movements brought forth many smiles; our dancing was in keeping with the formality of the event and honoring to the family.

In addition to the Thai friends we made, there were some remarkable "foreigners" who lived permanently in the city with whom we formed friendships. Two Americans stand out.

One was Maxine North. She and her screenwriter husband had gone to Thailand in 1950, because he specialized in stories with exotic locales. When he died only a few years later from polio, she decided to remain in the country.

Appalled by the way people either scooped up canal water, caught rainwater, or used unclean tap water, Mrs. North began a company called Polaris to market safe bottled water. Those who could afford it bought their drinking water from her company (as we did), and the glass bottles were delivered to their homes. It was a hard sell but slowly caught on.

The company's success increased later when many Americans came to the country during the Vietnam War. *Polaris* became almost synonymous with bottled water in Thailand. Maxine went on to pioneer other businesses in her adopted country. She was fluent in the language, so much so that she often acted as a key negotiator on behalf of the Thais.

Another such friend was a man named Jim Thompson. Bob and Jim had a great deal in common through their affiliation with the CIA as well as their involvement with the Thais. During World War II, Jim had served with the OSS (Office of Strategic Services), the forerunner of the CIA.

> In August 1945, Thompson was about to be sent into Thailand, when the Surrender of Japan officially ended World War II. He arrived in Thailand shortly after Victory over Japan Day and organized the Bangkok OSS office. . . . Thompson used his contacts with the Free Thai and Free Lao groups to gather information and defuse conflicts on Thailand's borders.
>
> —*Wikipedia*

Jim, like Maxine, fell in love with the country and stayed on to make his home in Bangkok. Almost single-handedly he revitalized the Thai silk industry in the 1950s and '60s, bringing it to worldwide attention. A great boost to the business was the release of the movie *The King and I* in 1956, which utilized Thai silks in the costumes.

> Besides inventing the bright jewel tones and dramatic color combinations today associated with Thai silk, he raised thousands of Thailand's poorest people out of poverty. His determination to keep his company cottage-based was significant for the women who made up the bulk of his work force. By allowing them to work at home, they retained their position in the household while becoming breadwinners.
>
> *—Wikipedia*

Through observing Jim's efforts, my appreciation for the phenomenal art and workmanship of the Thais grew. I found myself enjoying even more the richness of my surroundings. It was truly a luxury to be living among these extraordinary people.

Now—some fifty plus years later—I think I can finally tell about my own role with the CIA, that is, beyond that of clandestine wife.

One evening at our home, two men visiting us drew me into a conversation about photography. Was I interested in it? Would it be something I might like to have as a hobby? Their questions interested me, because I did like photography and did want to learn more. It was such a shame to be in the midst of this unique culture with such spectacular sights and not be able to capture them, not to mention that our three growing girls were irresistible subjects. So in no time, the men had me fully engaged in the conversation.

It turned out that their motive was to train me to become proficient in photography in order to competently use a darkroom and develop pictures—for their purposes. They told me I could have personal use of the excellent equipment they would set up. In fact, they wanted me to do that—it would be my cover. I was to practice my new hobby well so that I would become skilled and able to help the agents in their search for vital information.

Our garage became a developing studio. It consisted of a darkroom as well as a small waiting area with comfortable seating for the photographers whose pictures I was developing—day or night. A thick, black, ceiling-to-floor curtain separated the two sections. I developed their photos as needed, sometimes enlarging small segments of an image. These I would then piece together into one very large picture.

I did this for over a year, thoroughly enjoying the work. It gave me an outlet that was purposeful and fun and made me more a part of Bob's world.

As you can see, I did utilize my new camera and newfound skills to take delightful pictures. We used this one for our Christmas card that year.

The CIA assignment reached its natural conclusion in 1959, and Bob's tour in Bangkok was over. They wanted him to go to Kuala Lumpur, Malaysia, next, but he decided to turn down that assignment. Kuala Lumpur at that time was rather undeveloped and not a desirable place to raise children. Nina was fourteen; Nancy, twelve; and Deb was four. We thought it best to return to the States, to Virginia.

Leaving Thailand had its own element of sadness. We would miss the many enjoyable times we had shared as a family, exploring and learning about the Thai countryside. Time and again, its beauty had beckoned, and we had responded—always ready for a spontaneous picnic stop.

The Thais had welcomed us with such warmth, enriching us greatly by freely sharing their culture and customs with us. We had grown close to many, and we all hoped our lives would intersect again. Indeed, they would.

Chapter 6

Washington, DC
Laos
Bangkok

US Normalcy, Then Off Again

$\mathcal{B}$ack in the DC area, we found just the right home for rent in nearby Arlington, Virginia, in a cul-de-sac close to the Potomac. We stayed there three years (1959–1962), long enough to get grounded again and elated to be back on home turf.

The schools were good. Nina graduated from high school during our time there. We made new friends and joined a church where we felt at home. The church was Presbyterian, and its activities were uplifting. The five of us were all baptized in a large group, which included astronaut John Glenn and his family. He was also the girls' youth leader, and Nina learned to water ski from him.

John was one of our pioneer astronauts. Interacting with him on a personal level added a great deal to our interest in the Space Race and everything it meant to our country. On February 20, 1962, he flew the Friendship 7 mission, becoming the first American to orbit the earth and the fifth person in space.

> The Space Race was a 20th-century (1955–1972) competition between two Cold War rivals, the Soviet Union (USSR) and the United States (US), for supremacy in spaceflight capability. The technological superiority required for such supremacy was seen as necessary for national security, and symbolic of ideological superiority.
>
> —*Wikipedia*

Even though we were stateside, unique mementos of our travels were now part of our home. From Saipan we still had our glass ball collection, as well as a very large sea turtle shell, about three-feet in diameter. Our lifeguard, Enrique, from Tanapag Beach, had given it to us after he had prepared a special turtle soup dinner for his family.

And what were we to do with an enormous turtle shell in Virginia? Besides being decorative, it was perfect to use as a sturdy saucer-sled on the snow-banked slopes behind our home. I doubt Enrique ever imagined that the children would be so delighted by his gift many years later in the USA.

Although the snow was a thrilling experience for the kids, the weather was an obstacle for Bob. Finding his government career at a stalemate, he resigned from the CIA to try real estate again. However, that first winter had the worst snow in years, so it was impossible even to show houses, much less sell them. He tried other avenues of employment but found himself frustrated and restless.

Bob began to contemplate business possibilities that had occurred to him while we were in Thailand. There he had been struck by the public's drastic need for safe drinking water. Where there is need, there is often room for opportunity. Innovators, such as North and Thompson, were his inspiration. His imagination and ideas began to gain momentum and grew into a serious desire to make pure water widely accessible in Bangkok for office buildings, drinking fountains, swimming pools, and homes.

In spite of seeking investment money from every side, only one small investment came our way. I could not see how this dream of Bob's would work. He was so sure, and I was so unsure. To Bob, his plan meant vision and purpose; to me, it meant our world was crumbling.

Not only were we glaringly under-financed, but I could clearly see the implications to the children's schooling, especially Nina's. She would remain in the States to attend college. Our plan had been for her to get her degree at the University of Southern California (USC). But following Bob's dream, we would be able to keep her in college for her first year only. Even worse in my mind was that our little family would be split up, halfway around the world from each other. We were at a critical crossroad.

I had previously had doubts about Bob's other career decisions, but had also had faith in him. First, there had been his re-enlistment with the marines during the Korean conflict; then there had been his recruitment by the CIA and our assignment to Saipan. But this time my inner conflict was magnified exponentially, and my objections detracted from the good he was trying to accomplish.

Finally, Bob looked me straight in the eye and gave me an ultimatum: join him in the plan, or he would go it alone. It was a time of inner turmoil like nothing I had experienced before.

Again I searched within and struggled to know the best path for the family. In the end, there was no question where my stand should be—right by the side of my husband. I accepted Bob's wishes and told him I would support him. My priorities were in order; our family was more precious to me than security.

That was the leading hand of God. I do not take credit for it, because my doubts and fears were too great this time. It was God's strength that enabled me to make that commitment.

We sold everything we didn't absolutely have to have from our house in Virginia, putting every cent we had into Bob's dream. It was hard work to organize all this, as I wanted to make sure that we netted the most we could from the sale.

Parting with each item felt as though I was being reshaped somehow, bit by bit. Actually I think I was learning a lesson that comes the hard way. It's one thing to lose everything through a natural disaster, another to lose it by choice. Yet I shall never regret my choice; the basis was love.

> God, I see that you were preparing me to be content—regardless of my possessions, or lack of same, and regardless of my circumstances.

Nina would still do her first year at USC. We left Virginia and drove to the West Coast to get her settled into her new life. We stayed for three months over the summer in Irvine Terrace in Corona del Mar, while Bob continued his attempts to raise money and research the best source of equipment for his water purification venture. He needed a company with the appropriate engineering capabilities that would also be willing to work with him in Thailand.

Eventually he formed an association with an American water filtration company that promised custom solutions and were willing to expand into Bangkok. They seemed to understand and get on board with Bob's concept to make pure water available in Bangkok via tap water filtration units. The company would supply the equipment; Bob would be their rep in the Far East. We were on the move.

Bob went to Bangkok ahead of us to begin laying the groundwork for the business and our arrival. I followed soon after with Nancy and Debby, braced for the twenty-four hour trip and for the unknowns ahead. While in my heart I supported Bob in following his dream, I won't deny that my thoughts frequently gave way to doubts about its success. For a wife, that is a hard place to be.

It was also a very hard place for a mother to be. I was leaving my oldest daughter thousands of miles behind in the States and returning to Southeast Asia with two young girls, now fifteen and seven. This was 1962. The region was significantly more unsettled, to say the least, than it had been during our last period in Bangkok. Moreover, this time we had very little financial backing or stability, no government support, and no way to finance a trip home.

From the beginning, Bob's efforts to establish the pure water business in Thailand presented insurmountable obstacles; however, he was not one to give up easily. He was tenacious and had an all-consuming need to provide for his family while accomplishing something worthwhile. But that business was one that required dependability and cooperation beyond himself. It was essential that his supplier come through as promised. Bob would obtain the clients, only to find repeatedly that the company was simply not fulfilling their side of the bargain. They were inexperienced in doing business in Southeast Asia and proved to be inadequate for that time and place. Even the orders they did ship were improperly filled.

Had we had the capital that was necessary for a project of this scale, we might have endured the slow start. Perhaps eventually Bob and the supplier could have solved the issues plaguing them. But without financial depth, the business was doomed from the start. It was awful for Bob, and it was awful for me to see him floundering and watch the inevitable.

Since the girls were enrolled once again at the newly built International School, I set about looking for a job that would allow me to be home in time for their return from school. I found a position immediately with Sverdrup & Parcel Engineering, an American company based out of St. Louis. They had built the famous Yanhee Dam and the East-West Highway in Thailand.

To my surprise, I liked the job. It was a busy office. Days there were challenging because of the precision required of me, but not unpleasant. By typing up briefs, I learned a great deal about the intricate and exacting science of engineering.

There was a tier system to the pay scale of large American companies operating there. Topmost were those who were brought over to Bangkok from the States for the express purpose of working with them. Next were the local Thais. There was a third level of political hiring. The fourth and bottom level was Americans who lived locally, like me.

In stark contrast to our former life in Bangkok, I rode a crowded bus to and from work. Firsthand I felt the stigma applied by eyes that saw me as downtrodden, not worth very much. Thankfully I didn't internalize that. I doubt I could have expressed this at the time, but while the prejudice was sobering, I developed a deeper understanding and empathy for people.

Matters of daily life demanded intense effort on my part. We were living on my salary alone. And we were virtually on our own. We had no access to the PX, commissary, or US Post Office. We shopped at the local market stalls.

A bright light was our one servant who was a big help with the cleaning, washing, and ironing. She was sweet and so cheerful that I still think of her with appreciation. Her name was a source of shy pride and giggles to her. It was pronounced Oosa and spelled Usa. Whether it was her given name or a name she thought was cute to adopt for herself, we'll never know.

A year or more passed until Bob began to face the huge toll that the strain of his repeated failures was taking on him. He would later admit, even to others, that he came to a point of pure despondency. Despair. I thank God that we went through this trial together with complete openness— that we trusted each other implicitly.

Almost objectively, he debated with himself out loud the pros and cons of which method of death would be preferable, jumping off the bridge or getting a gun and shooting himself. I know beyond a doubt that his love for me and his three young daughters stopped him. He described haunting thoughts of us left alone to pick up the pieces in a foreign country with no insurance or funds of any kind. It is also not beyond the realm of possibility that an angel of the Lord stayed his hand.

One day during this dark season, Bob came to me and broke the news that he had been offered a job in Laos. It was dangerous and would mean his being separated from us for at least three months without contact of any kind, but he could not refuse it. Our good friend Dutch Brongersma, of Saipan days, wanted Bob to assist him with the rapidly growing Bird Air Transport in Vientiane, Laos. The decision had to be yes.

This was a terrible time for me; however, thankfully the girls were unaware, as we managed to keep up our routine while Dad was "away on business."

At this point, I think it is important to insert the historical backdrop so that even those readers who may have been intently watching and reading American news during this period of our lives in Southeast Asia (1962–69) can put this part of my story into the bigger picture. The American news media could not tell everything. They were greatly restricted, and properly so, from expressing the facts of America's covert activities beyond the borders of Vietnam. It was safer for those performing undercover services, as well as for the country, to keep the news focused on the Vietnam arena and its casualties.

Bob's work in Vientiane directly involved him with the plight of the Hmong tribes in the valley of Long Cheng, often described as "the most secret place on earth"—an apt place for staging what became known as the Secret War of Laos. Hmong guerrilla soldiers, under the charismatic leadership of General Vang Pao and with the support of the CIA, waged grueling war against the invading communists (Pathet Lao). Long Cheng would develop into the epicenter of the American-Hmong war effort.

The Hmong were endearing and genuinely friendly to us, sharing their homes and deeply held customs. To gain insight into their culture was a rare privilege. Their textiles were exceptional and reflected their ancestry with significant colors and designs. They are proud, independent, and loyal people.

There was a great deal involved to supply the extensive humanitarian, manpower, and armament needs of the Hmong. A key figure to both the Hmong and the Americans who became a close friend of ours was Edgar "Pop" Buell. He was a humble farmer from Indiana who, after becoming widowed, joined the International Voluntary Services (a precursor to the Peace Corps). He lived in a simple hut among the Hmong, was a huge advocate for their well-being, and was dearly loved.

Bob's job was with Bird Air Transport, a fledgling enterprise started by Bill Bird. Bill had spent years on runway projects and other rebuilding efforts in Panama and the Philippines. He had gone out to Laos to negotiate work on the runway for Wattay Airport, near the Laotian capital of Vientiane. Bill's heart was in planes themselves and all that went along with planes for hire in a war zone.

The air war in Laos was intensifying. Increasingly governments and businesses were in need of more rapid, small air support; however, all such contracts were going to the CIA's Air America without a bidding process. The time was right to supply the additional air power required by the United States in that region of Southeast Asia. After overcoming US political obstacles to obtain competing bidding rights, he launched Bird Air.

Expecting to get his first contract, Bill bought an old US military trainer plane that had been converted into a transport plane. Its long-time pilot had been R. L. "Dutch" Brongersma, who was hired as an essential part of the deal to buy the plane. Dutch became chief of operations and immediately contacted Bob about joining him. Their past association had fostered deep respect and friendship between the two of them.

Dutch had been a marine pilot in World War II who gained his early flight experience maneuvering on and off storm-tossed carrier decks. Early in the war, he had flown for Civil Air Transport (CAT), an airline started by General Claire Chennault to implement CIA relief operations to Chinese nationalists and to take the general wherever he needed to go.

Dutch's exploits were legend: flying mysterious airdrops across northern Burma to Tibet, undercover operations into China, and mercy missions to remote hill tribes. Within the air world, Dutch held the reputation of being the best freelance pilot in Asia.

He was salty and tough yet completely a gentleman. His wife, Anita, was a westernized Chinese beauty. It baffled me how she could stand the tensions of his risk-taking life, but they found each other and needed and loved each other.

Bob's qualities complemented Dutch's for this operation. Bob had steady leadership abilities and a keen understanding of the wild bunch of pilots as well as the local people he had to recruit. He also possessed a fearless willingness to do whatever it took to get the job done. The two were a perfect match, and Bill Bird's charter air service literally took off.

> (Bird Air) was a freewheeling international air service of hair-raising flying feats and unbelievable pilots, a bareknuckle operation that hauled cargo, jungle commandoes, rice bags and secret agents into and out of the wilds of Laos. It was a fitting name. Only a bird could land on some of the strips that Bird Air pilots used. These runways were cocked at crazy angles on mountainsides, with L-shaped bends in the middle of some, others barely 75 feet long and carved out of opium-poppy fields bursting with red, purple and white blooms. The line began as a shoestring operation, but it would grow big enough to conduct an airlift that rescued hundreds of frantic refugees during the collapse of Saigon in 1975.

> —*Soldiers of Fortune by Sterling Seagrave*

Bird Air later would also be instrumental in the escape of the loyal Hmong after the Pathet Lao took control. That history is vividly recounted in the book *Sky Is Falling (An Oral History of the CIA's Evacuation of the Hmong from Laos)* by Gayle L. Morrison, an admirer and supporter of the Hmong people.

I shall try to impart to you what it was like to be on the other end of that action during those first months without contact from Bob. In a word, I felt exposed. There I was, a foreign woman with two young children in Bangkok, alone, with no visible husband. What no one knew, but what I knew all too well, was why he wasn't with me. While I didn't have all the facts, I knew he had to be in the midst of the war for freedom versus communism raging just over the Thai border.

It was a given that his life was in constant danger. And so were our lives in danger. There were never-ending threats of communist incursion into Thailand. Rumors of imminent attacks on Bangkok ran rampant in the workplace around me, in the markets, and in what news I could glean. Fear stalked me. I feared for Bob. I feared for the girls. And, I must admit, I felt extremely vulnerable in my aloneness.

One day I learned that an old friend of Bob's and mine was visiting the American embassy in Bangkok. I desperately wanted hard news about our situation. I had no one to turn to. I could not confide in anyone. But this friend went back far with Bob and me through work with the CIA, and I knew I could trust him.

I contacted him and said I urgently needed to talk to him. He agreed and invited me to meet him at his hotel. Because I felt the need for privacy, I went to his room, where I could cry openly, expose my fears, and ask all my questions. He was very reassuring, telling me that he would alert me to any sudden Thai military action.

What a relief I felt, at last being able to let down my brave façade and to know that at least an agreement of forewarning had been set in place. I left better equipped to keep on going while I waited for Bob to get back to see us.

At last Bob was able to make a short trip to Bangkok and to hold us in his arms. As we caught each other up on news, I told him about meeting our friend. I had no hesitation in telling him, as it was part of how my side of the story had progressed. Never had it dawned on me how that encounter would feel to Bob. He was incredibly hurt. It was painful for him to realize that he had caused me to feel so vulnerable and scared that I had needed to turn to another man for security.

It was his pride that was hurt, I think, more than anything else, because his reason for having taken the job with Bird Air was that he had failed with his water-filtration business. His self-esteem took another low blow, and it was his beloved wife who had dealt it. I was mortified. Horrified really. I was hurt. He was hurt. It colored that time with an undermining doubt that shook us both severely.

Gradually we both took deep breaths from the initial shock of this rift, realizing there was nothing severe enough for harbored hard feelings. We were both safe, and the girls were safe, so we just needed to move on. Fortunately, there was not the luxury of time to nurse our wounds.

What do I think about that episode now? Not in terms of regretting my actions certainly, as there's no need to defend my seeking out this friend in a time of crisis. Rather, I think more in terms of how easy it is for two people who love each other to inflict pain on each other unwittingly. Bob and I had been living through an enforced separation, and separation in itself represents sad times for any couple. While apart, we were each subjected to different forms of extreme stress that tended to make us react individually from our own centers of weakness.

As I look into the wisdom of God's Word, I see where we are taught to always put others before ourselves and God before all. Had Bob and I reflected beforehand on what we each had to endure alone, we might have reacted with greater sensitivity and understanding for the other when we met again. Love—not accusations and frustrations—would have been the healing oil. I would not have been the stressed wife failing to take into account Bob's wounds, and Bob would not have been the proud man unable to listen to his faithful wife. Yet, when all was said and done, Bob and I were stronger for the battle. That's the way it is with tough times—handled with care, we grow in character.

Although Bob and Dutch's small office was at the airport in Vientiane, Bob lived just outside the city in the company's compound, which Bill Bird had built largely, I venture to say, from questionably acquired concrete. The compound was a spacious, inviting facility amid grassy, flowered gardens. A number of separate, well-appointed apartments of varying sizes for pilots and visitors surrounded a forty-foot swimming pool, which remained steadily filled with fresh well water. At first Bill did not want wives in Laos, but after a while the girls and I flew up regularly in one of the company's small aircraft to be with Bob. How we anticipated those visits!

Below is a photo of us, basking on what could easily pass for a sandy beach—but this is land-locked Laos (background). We are on its border with Thailand (not in the photo), lying on the sandy bottom of the Mekong River, no doubt reminiscing about our beaches in California and wondering when we would see them again. During the monsoon season, the rains would swell the river all the way to the top of its steep bank, often overflowing it. In the dry season, the river then dropped to reveal this fine white sand.

The flights going up to the compound could be terrifying, to say the least, for we had to fly over thickly jungled terrain through sheer cliffs. There was a time when Nancy went up by herself to see her dad; Debby and I, for some reason, couldn't go.

Bob arranged for her to ride up in one of the six-seater, two-engine planes. Over northern Thailand, in heavy clouds with no visibility, one engine failed. Nancy remembers vividly how scared she was. The plane jerked repeatedly to the right as the pilot tried in vain to restart the engine. Without visible land or sky, the effect was disorienting. Finally the pilot managed to bring the disabled plane down onto a dirt field for an unstable, shaky—but safe—landing. All in a day's work for the pilot, but certainly memorable for Nancy. Another plane soon arrived in its place to continue the trip.

One of my experiences going up to the compound did not end as well for the pilot. Deb and I were traveling together. The plane was a new one (not uncommon, as the number of crashes created a steady need for new planes). We were over the Mekong in the dry season, flying very low. The pilot, with a bit of the show-off in him, was eager to test the capabilities of the new plane. Tipping the plane sideways, he skimmed along the steep cliff at ninety degrees. Debby was speechlessly terrified.

When we landed, Bob was waiting for us. I was still all aglow and breathless as I told Bob of our adventure, expecting him to be glad for me. Instead, he was furious. He fired the pilot then and there for violating the rules against unnecessary risk-taking. There was ample enough of that without extra stunts—not to mention he had jeopardized his wife's and daughter's lives.

Not just anybody who could fly a small plane was cut out for the dangerous missions flown in this terrain, which in itself was an even a greater threat than enemy fire. The ones who did best had experience flying in Alaska or had worked as rescue or crop-duster pilots. They possessed the instincts to navigate in tight spots in unpredictable, fast-changing weather conditions. The cargos they carried to the Hmong were referred to as light or heavy loads. Light drops were rice and supplies; heavy drops were military arms. The number of men on board depended on the mission. Besides the cargo handlers, there were times when agents had to parachute strategically within the zone.

The pilots were all daredevils, nervy but seasoned. They thrived on the smell of adventure and the good money they could make risking their lives. And most drank a lot. Socially an informal dual culture emerged: the loners who pretty much kept to themselves and the rowdy bunch who preferred to roughhouse at The Green Latrine.

The wild stories emanating from there made me very curious to witness it firsthand. I teased Bob to take me there, but needless to say, he would hear nothing of it. He held stiff reins on the men, including a twelve-hour rule, which referred to the time from "bottle to throttle." The fellows respected him and knew he meant business, for their own good.

Crashes up-country brought with them stark reality. Those killed or injured were not always just the pilot and crew but also the cargo handlers, the dedicated locals. They were invaluable not merely for their muscle, but also for their intimate knowledge of the territory and the Mekong River. The river was their highway, their lifeline for commerce and daily needs. They traversed it routinely on their small barges to cross between Laos and Thailand.

Upon word of a crash, Bob would send a patrol to survey the wreckage and report back. It was mandatory to destroy everything—documents as well as the remains of the planes themselves. Any wounded or dead had to be returned to the Vientiane airport. It was a shock to me to learn that there were occasions when body bags had to be left in Bob's office, awaiting proper assessment of circumstances prior to release.

Sometimes Bob would include himself in the patrols to the wreckage site, but there came a day when the pilot assigned stood firm and refused take him along—Bob was simply too old (about forty-five) for the rigors of the jungle. That pierced Bob to the core. He thought he was ageless and still saw himself as an indomitable marine.

Of course, he recognized that his main focus had to be management and logistics, and certainly his plate was full, but he did miss the direct involvement. Early each morning he dispatched mission crews—counting them out, counting them in. After reviewing their reports on the enemy and what the Hmong tribesmen needed, he set in motion the resulting series of tasks, which had to be executed with precision, taking into consideration every variable. All the while, he made sure to keep US Ambassador Sullivan in Vientiane abreast of operations.

Our world was not confined to Vientiane or Bangkok. Nina was in California and about to be married—to a man we had never met.

Her fiancé was Paul, a fellow student at USC. He was soon to graduate and receive his much-sought-after commission in the navy. He and Nina were determined to marry and often considered elopement, but that would have meant losing his commission. Paul's mother, Loretto, who had worked hard to see that her son receive officer ranking, was adamant that they not elope, as was I. It was reassuring to know that even before meeting Loretto, she and I were already in agreement.

The wedding day plan was tight: graduation was to be in the morning; the wedding and reception, that afternoon. All was set for the big day. Except for one thing—we were clear across the world with very little money to get back. We made the hard decision that only I would attend, though it deeply saddened us that Bob would miss his first daughter's wedding.

My journey to the wedding alone turned into a little story in itself. Bob managed a way home for me through his many airline contacts. In my best Thai silk suit, I boarded a JAL plane from Bangkok to Tokyo. I stayed at the Imperial Hotel overnight, then got the super-fast train the next morning for the Tachikawa US Air Base some distance out of town. To say we passengers were tightly jammed in that train is a major understatement.

Reaching my last stop, I managed to twist myself off the train and became instantly overwhelmed by a sea of Japanese, each busily scurrying to work or other equally compelling destination. Trying to orient myself, I was standing still and standing out—like a misplaced, tall, white statue.

Out of nowhere, a big, good-looking, take-charge American soldier came up to me. "Do you need help, Ma'am?"

Boy, did I! I couldn't even see how to get off the platform.

He said he had a car waiting to go to the base with several officers, and there was one available seat in the back. Off we went. I had no identification to get on the base, but they all showed theirs, and we were waved through the gate.

It was late afternoon, so I made my way to the Officers Club. While families were laughing and dining, I sat alone with a small meal and watched quietly, my anticipation mixed with a bit of melancholy. I took my suitcase to the ladies' room and changed into warm slacks. Instructions were to go clear across the field to where the cargo flights took off.

When I found my plane, the crew were grumbling to themselves about bad luck. Apparently I was the bad luck: a female passenger on an empty cargo flight—bad omen. They placed me on a discarded bench seat and at least gave me a warm army blanket. There I huddled, staring at the long, empty, cold cargo tunnel for the night. We flew way north in order to make good time. I could see the ice packed on the wings. But we did make record time—ten hours.

It was almost midnight when I deplaned in San Francisco and rushed to the PSA window that was to close at midnight. Having no place to stay overnight and with wedding plans the next day, I had to make that last plane. It happened that the movie star Buddy Rogers and his entourage were ahead of me. Buddy took pity on me and my plight and let me go ahead of him. After him, the counter closed.

Landing at LAX, I took a shuttle to the train station downtown, where I found a taxi to take me to Nina's apartment. Nina had been working in an office on Wilshire Boulevard and living with her cousin, Dew, in an apartment near work. The two of them were not just related but great friends.

I told the driver my mission, and he went on and on about young kids nowadays shacking up. "Not mine!" I protested. He took my bag to the apartment door and rang.

Who should answer but Paul and another cousin Bill, both in skivvies! The driver just shook his head and left, more convinced than ever.

Even though it was two in the morning, Nina, Dew, and I were so excited about seeing each other after our long separation and the expectations of the next day that the time mattered little. As we discussed plans, the fellows got in on the act too. It seems that they had had to move from their apartment, so the gals had offered to help them out for the night with a place to stay. That's how I met my future first son-in-law. We laugh about it still.

Early the next day, the plan was on. The first stop was Hemet to meet Paul's mother. I found Loretto to be a kind, capable, gracious lady. She was known for her delicious cooking and homemaking talents.

The graduation ceremony at USC was grand and touching at the same time. Later we assembled in the pastor's office of the Institute of Religious Science on Sixth Street for the wedding ceremony. This was the church Mother had introduced us to and which Nina had continued to attend.

Afterward Grandma Florence (Bob's mother) had us all over to her lovely home on Lido Isle for the wedding reception with many family members present. Shortly the newlyweds were off to report to duty in Bremerton, Washington. I visited a little longer and then caught my planned flight home on Pan Am to Bangkok to recount my adventure to eager, curious ears.

The following year, Nancy graduated from International School Bangkok. One of the big school projects each year was to publish a real yearbook. With no such thing as a photography studio to go to for a graduation picture, we were directed to a vendor who was set up outdoors along a bustling street in the middle of town. The photographer proudly produced a black drape, which we realized would be used by all the senior girls for their formal blouse. After snapping Nancy's picture, he vanished into his makeshift dark room—black material hung over scaffolding.

We left him to his film and pans of developing solution, later returning to find the end result—perfect.

Nancy had her sights set on the University of California, Santa Barbara. She was almost eighteen. Although we would have loved to fly home with her and get her settled in college, it was not feasible. So we arranged for her to travel on a chartered flight with a group of missionaries going from Bangkok to London. The trip would include a two-day visit to the Holy Land, which turned out to be very special to her.

Once they arrived in London, Nancy was on her own for two days of sightseeing before flying off to Boston. The plan was for her to buy an airline ticket from Boston to Idaho, where she would visit for the summer with Nina and Paul. Instead, she took a Greyhound bus all the way—a change we learned about well after the fact.

Now Nancy says that bus trip taught her how naive, vulnerable, and young she really was, and that maybe it wasn't her best idea. But at that time she was confident in her new endeavors and basked in her independence. She certainly had Bob's spirit of adventure. It was amazing to see our own characteristics reflected in our children. So, though there was sadness in her being so far away, I smile to think perhaps it was we who had given her wings.

Not too long after Nancy headed to college, Deb and I left Bangkok to live at the compound in Laos with Bob. It was definitely hard on Debby not having Nancy there. I missed having my two eldest nearby, but it was great that at least Deb and I could be with Bob.

There was an International School in Vientiane where we enrolled Deb. Soon she had a best friend, Denise, who looked and acted so much like her they could have been twins. They were inseparable. That friendship made a big difference for her.

I cherish something Debby wrote to me in 2010 about that time in her life: "Mom, you taught me to search for the love of God. My testimony of God really was solidified at that little Christian church in Vientiane, Laos, when the Sunday school teacher gave me a card with Proverbs 3:5-6 on it: 'Trust in the Lord with all your heart, and lean not unto your own understanding; in all your ways acknowledge him, and he shall direct your paths.' Thank you for dragging me there even though it was tough."

During our Vientiane period, a news event in March of 1967 affected us deeply. Jim Thompson, of Thai Silk fame, was reported missing and feared dead. He had become one of the most famous Americans living in Asia. The local newspapers ran the story, day after day. So much mystery surrounded it that it seemed the investigation just made the matter more confusing.

His disappearance was never explained, and his body was never found. There was serious speculation that his undercover ties were at the heart of the matter. We never knew. Regardless, we were shaken and grieved for our friend.

> Thompson was unlike any other figure in Southeast Asia. He was an American, an ex-architect, a retired army officer, a one-time spy, a silk merchant and a renowned collector of antiques. Most of his treasures, if not all, were amassed after he came to Thailand. In 1958, he began what was to be the pinnacle of his architectural achievement—the construction of a new home to showcase his *objects d'art*.
>
> —*Wikipedia*

That home, the Jim Thompson House, was turned into a museum and is still available for tours.

The success of Bird Air Transport caught the attention of Bob Six, president of Continental Airlines (CAL), who wanted a presence in the region with an eye toward future air routes in Southeast Asia. Besides that, Six was fascinated by the *Terry and the Pirates* world of the undercover war. He bought out Bird and Sons and visited the compound many times with his charming wife, Audrey Meadows. She was the costar with Jackie Gleason in the sitcom series *The Honeymooners*. To accommodate their frequent visits, they maintained a residence in one of the apartment suites at our newly christened Continental Compound.

Bob Six and my Bob really connected, and so when Continental took over operations, Six made him assistant manager of the new subsidiary company, Continental Air Services (CAS), with Dutch in Laos. His boss was Ed Cotter, Audrey's brother. My unofficial role was to arrange social activities on behalf of Continental, something that came easily to me.

The Sixes were an unmistakable couple, both very tall, striking people; both possessed booming voices and tremendous senses of humor. There was never a dull moment with them around. They brought many well-known visitors with them on their frequent trips to the compound. Among them were such dignitaries as Robert Kennedy, attorney general under his brother, John, and later US Senator from New York; Pierre Salinger, White House press secretary to John Kennedy and Lyndon Johnson, later US Senator from California, and then campaign manager for Robert Kennedy; and Henry Kissinger, national security adviser to Nixon.

In the picture below, Debby was ready to travel with the Salingers and the Sixes to Vientiane from Bangkok on the CAS plane. From the left are Pierre, Debby, Audrey and Bob Six, and Nicole Salinger.

Audrey and I spent a lot of time together and became close, enjoying each other a great deal. She had an infectious laugh, was without pretense, and very easy to like. At informal times, she didn't mind in the least walking around with her hair in curlers—not unlike the Alice character in *The Honeymooners'*. However, she was always sharp socially. I remember one typical comment she made to me. With her mouth shielded behind her hand, she whispered, "Now, Sue, I want you to introduce me to everyone I should meet. Don't let me turn on my charm to someone's driver."

She delighted in the intricate skill that went into the silks made locally. Together she and I spent hours shopping in all the wonderful nooks and crannies with a purpose: she had decided to furnish their Arizona ranch home completely with the rare beauty of Far Eastern art and Thai silks. Later, when that home was destroyed by fire, she turned to me to find and ship the exact items needed to begin again. I valued that trust and our relationship.

I organized many of Continental's dinners and receptions, which often included the ambassador and his wife and others from the embassy in Vientiane. It was a friendly, close-knit family of Americans with a common goal to represent America well. But our intent was not to be insular—there was an exceptional group of Thais and Laotians we got to know and appreciate who certainly enriched our lives.

Our parties were sometimes at the compound, which the ambassador and his wife enjoyed visiting, especially when it was one of our relaxed curry dinners set up outside on the cool grass. At other times, the events were at the American embassy itself or some other suitable venue.

One particular night stands out for its beauty—and hilarity. The event was staged at a hotel in Bangkok. Pierre Salinger was visiting just at the time of a spaceship launching. To honor the occasion, the hotel created two impressive ice sculptures set on a large table: one was a sleek, imposing Continental plane; next to it was a gleaming spaceship, tall and proud, ready to blast off. There was no denying that the spaceship looked for all the world like a giant phallic symbol.

As the party progressed and the room warmed, we embarrassingly noticed the gradual melting of the once erect spaceship. One timid titter started it, and then another, until the whole room filled to bursting with contagious belly laughs. I don't think the queen herself could have kept a straight face.

Throughout our time in Vientiane, there was the constant backdrop of war with the communist Pathet Lao who were determined to overtake the country. There was also a constant threat of disease. Bob and I got dengue fever— twice. Like malaria, dengue is transmitted by mosquitoes, of which there was no shortage.

Since minimal medical help was available, it was somehow reassuring to have a partner in misery. There we were, the two of us wracked with fever, lying side by side in our big bed. We were so sick that even to move a little finger required the utmost concentration. Thank goodness Deb was well and that she was there to help. Without her help and that of a most capable servant, we would have been in trouble.

> *Though I walk through the valley of the shadow of death, I will fear no evil; for you are with me; your rod and your staff, they comfort me (Psalm 23:4).*

Beyond illness, we had three other close calls. On one occasion, the attack occurred while Bob and I were driving back to the compound after a party at a pilot's home outside Vientiane. We were traveling on a road next to the wall of a *wat* (Buddhist monastery-temple). A gunman hiding behind the wall shot directly at us. I could feel the bullet's speed as it whizzed past my head. Bob yelled, "Hit the floor!" No need;

I was already there. He got me safely home, then returned to the scene to search for the bullet, hoping to learn who was behind the attack. After finding out what he could, he headed back to the pilot's house to phone in a report.

The second incident occurred when Nina had come out to visit us. Bob was escorting her home after a formal party at the Ambassador's residence. They were in a small jeep on a narrow side street when a barricade set up by the Pathet Lao forced them to stop. It was the blackest of nights. Suddenly a soldier popped up and shoved a rifle at Nina. Bob jumped out, showed ID, and somehow managed to talk the guy into letting them go.

The last directly life-threatening event occurred one night when we were at our home, which was between the airport and downtown Vientiane. A skirmish erupted from both points: the Pathet Lao from the center of the city and the Laotian Army from the airport. Artillery fire streaked over our house for what seemed an eternity. We were in the rockets' red glare all right.

Bob Six's goals of establishing air routes in Southeast Asia included promoting tourism to the Pacific islands of Micronesia and the Marianas. He created Air Micronesia, a subsidiary company of Continental, and asked Bob to be the manager, operating out of a permanent office in Bangkok.

Although that meant our lives were largely back in Bangkok again, it also meant our making frequent trips to remote islands to carry out his vision. We still chuckle over these snapshots of Truk International Airport, with signs clearly directing "all" its passengers as to where to enter and where to pick up their bags.

Bob's work as manager was engrossing and intense, and, as his wife, I was expected again to handle social arrangements. We maintained close ties and strong affiliation with the Vientiane operation held down by Dutch, yet a new environment meant new people in our lives, adding interest and dimension.

We found that a number of these friends were also boating enthusiasts. It was a special weekend when we could get away from town and drive down the Gulf of Thailand to Pattaya Beach. Now it's a popular resort, but in the sixties, it was a rustic getaway. We families fixed up an old shack on the beach and dubbed it, tongue in cheek, the Royal Varuna Yacht Club. To signify and dignify the "immense status" of membership, each sailboat owner was given a handsome loving cup (of clay), which bore the name of their boat. We called our fifteen-footer the *Deborah Ann*.

One very sunny day, there was enough breeze for a good sailing race, and eight families assembled on the beach ready to set up sails. A small island off in the distance was the goal. The gun went off, and the competition was on. Deb and Bob raised the sails of the *Deborah Ann* and jockeyed for position. The seas were a bit choppy; the winds, perfect. The rest of us cheered them all from the sand. What a pretty sight!

Nearly at their turnaround point, a powerful, gusty wind sent Deb and Bob flying off into the warm water. The *Deborah Ann* whirled completely on its side, sails flat on the water's surface. With their life jackets on and treading water, Bob and Deb immediately attempted to right the boat, heavy sails and all. The committee boat sped off to the rescue while we gals watched in shock from the beach. Before the committee boat could arrive, the two of them had successfully righted the boat.

Bob was proud of Deb for not panicking and for crewing like a pro. Soon the two drenched but exhilarated "boatees" arrived safely on shore. I loved seeing their camaraderie as they shared that rare tropical adventure. And Debby learned firsthand that the greatest victory is not always in the win.

Keeping up with Nina and Nancy's fast-changing lives so far away became a never-ending challenge. Letter writing was our best form of communication. We girls enjoyed it, knowing the happiness that a letter being received on the other end would bring.

However, we were able to make a phone call, if necessary, and that was reassuring. The process of phone calls was primitive by modern standards. First, a reservation for the phone had to be made several days in advance; then came a trip to the post office to put in the call (which took a while); and then we'd do our level best to talk and hear over the static—at twelve dollars a minute. Translate that into today's money, and we were paying eighty-five dollars for sixty seconds! We made only one or two very short calls while there.

There were always surprises in the next letter. Moves were inevitable for Nina and Paul, due to their Navy life. Meanwhile, Nancy was energy personified. Her chosen field of nursing was perfect for her personality, and she put her all into studying at Kaiser School of Nursing in Oakland, California.

In 1968 thrilling plans were afoot for Nancy. She and her high school sweetheart, Gary, wanted to be married. They both had attended the International School in Bangkok, so we knew him well. Gary had also returned to the States and was attending Oregon State University's School of Forestry in Corvallis.

In January I flew to San Francisco from Bangkok for a short stay to help Nancy plan for their wedding in June. She picked me up at the airport in San Francisco in her little Volkswagen bug. While maneuvering the steep San Francisco hills, she casually mentioned that she had just learned how to drive a stick shift the day she bought the car—yesterday! Incredulous, but not entirely surprising. I howled with laughter. This was Nancy. There was a job to do, so she did it. We breezed on down to Newport, talking nonstop about plans.

Fortunately, in June we all could return to be there for their big day. The beautiful Presbyterian Church in Newport was the perfect setting with Rev. Derenfield officiating. Nina and Debby were Nancy's attendants; Gary's brother, David, the best man; Nolan's three sons were ushers; Nancy's sweet cousin, Alyce Dabney, the little flower girl.

Bob was absolutely beaming that day. Many times he declared how proud and sentimental he felt walking with his daughter on his arm down that long aisle.

By 1969 the air routes were well established, and Continental's Bangkok operation was running smoothly under Bob's direction. Bob Six offered Bob a promotion to be vice president of the Southeast Asia Region with CAL, headquartered in El Segundo, California.

Could it be? Could it really be that we were going back home for good? Yes!

Before returning to the States, we took advantage of the time we had between Bob's assignments to visit places we had heard a great deal about but had not yet seen. Our first stop was Burma, where an embassy friend met us. We toured the famous Shwedagon Pagoda together, and then he warmly entertained us with lunch at his tropical Burmese home. Normally Burma was a closed country to tourists, and even though we managed to be allowed in, their strict regulations permitted us to stay there no more than one day and evening.

By nightfall we were on a flight to Beirut, arriving for breakfast. Aside from a few tentative catnaps, since leaving Bangkok we had gone forty-five hours without sleep. Fourteen-year-old Deb was beyond tired. I think she felt her parents had finally gone over the edge.

We had just one day in Lebanon also, so we hired a taxi, determined to see as much as we could. We crossed the Lebanon Mountains into the vast Beqaa Valley, where we walked the ruins of a Baalbek temple, older than those in Greece. The lone caretaker there kindly agreed to give us a personal tour. It was fabulous, indeed, and huge even in the expansive terrain.

Back on the desolate desert road shared with occasional camels, we stopped at a tiny café where turbaned men were leisurely smoking water pipes as they ate what looked like shish kebabs. Outside we were intrigued by a small group of camels with drivers. The men invited us to approach their animals—and even to ride them. Bob had the sole triumph;

Deb and I were both hopeless. She and I tried gamely, only to slip off instantly down their smelly, bumpy, stubbly sides.

Finally back in Beirut, we got one night of marvelous sleep at the St. George Hotel. The city was exquisite. I hate to think of it as it is now, ravaged and scarred by conflicts.

Still our thirst for touring was not yet satiated. The next morning we were off to Frankfurt and traveled throughout Germany. It might have been exhausting, but Bob and I savored every moment.

As planned, Bob returned to Bangkok to wrap up business, and Deb and I headed home without him—minor in the scheme of things and not the least dampening to our spirits. We were all too busy relishing the idea that after a full eighteen years away, we were on our way home to our beloved California—for good. We had gone through incredible experiences together, yet we were still intact as a family. My cup was running over.

Chapter 7

NEWPORT BEACH
MISSION VIEJO
TAIPEI

Finally Home

*D*eb and I landed at LAX to an uproarious welcome. The whole family had converged to greet us. As I started walking, and the mist of happy tears began to clear from my eyes, I wanted to touch—even kiss—the ground itself, the ground of our country, our home that we had missed so much.

We had come ahead of Bob in order to enroll Deb at Corona del Mar High School, and he would be home for Christmas. She and I searched out real estate. We found a beautiful two-story condo on a green belt only one block from her school. I signed a lease option, awaiting Bob's okay to buy.

Actually Bob liked the condo but had objections to the air traffic noise. As soon as the lease was up, we three hunted again. We decided on a charming home in Irvine Terrace—a choice location nearer the ocean and across from Newport Center on Coast Highway. The street was called Serenade Terrace, totally appropriate to the romantic way we felt being there. The house had a swimming pool that promptly became the most popular gathering place for family and friends.

Enjoying our home as we did, Bob felt his long drive daily to LAX was well worth it. I tried to make our early morning routine as pleasing as I could for him, starting at six with his to-go breakfast of choice: toast, lots of butter, peanut butter on top of that, crisp bacon on the side, and coffee. Now I think of that and cringe, but who knew about proper diet then? He had a snappy apple-green convertible, which made his ride more fun. I can still see him looking back over his shoulder at me with a lovingly mischievous grin as he drove off, cigar poised to enjoy in the open air.

Our evenings had their rhythm too. He looked forward to the welcoming beach air, a swim every night, and our ritual martini before dinner. The meal would be ready and waiting. The table was set with candles or flowers, and savory kitchen aromas promised a dinner that I was pretty sure he would enjoy.

Bob made the most of having the magical title of vice president, kidding that he now had a key to the executive washroom. To complete his office as a VP, he wanted a picture of his wife on his desk.

I had only a casual snapshot to offer. When that wasn't good enough for him, I got dolled up and sat for a portrait. Here you have the touched-up me.

Debby did well in her high school work and extracurricular activities. Thanks to Auntie Mary, she became involved in the National Charity League, a service club. She and her classmates completed the required annual volunteer hours in the community.

After three years, a traditional awards event was given for her class. It was a formal debutante ball held at The Newporter. Perhaps the most to benefit were the mothers, for we had developed good friendships through our volunteer efforts to make the ball a success.

Debby presented herself most graciously but breathed a deep sigh of relief when the fuss was over.

She was about to graduate from high school, and we began the search for her choice of colleges in California and Oregon. Bob's family, back to his grandfather, had lived in Portland and had been well established in the community. She decided on the University of Portland, and although it would be far from us, we knew that with our Continental passes and discount privileges, she would be able to fly back and forth to Newport frequently.

While a freshman, she met and dated Andy, then a junior. Soon they were engaged to be married. That wedding was a bit complicated to plan, however, as Deb wanted very much to be married in Portland but at the same time wanted to use the family's special silver and brocade linens. As those items were all in Newport, we packed everything up and took the boxes with us on the plane. It was a tall order but made for enjoyable, bustling commotion.

The First United Methodist Church was the setting for the entire wedding, including the reception. The day was typically rainy for Portland, but no matter. Nina, Nancy, and I shopped the local stores, buying the cake, pretty sandwiches, punch, and other needed touches. The table was sparkling with silver gleaming, candles glowing, and punchbowl shimmering. This time it was precious Deb whom Bob walked down the aisle. Again, he was brimming with pride.

Our family was staying in the penthouse suite of the historic Benson Hotel, where we celebrated informally after the reception. The next day, as the bride and groom went off for their honeymoon, the rest of us caravanned home. On the way, we camped out at Castle Crags State Park, just south of Mount Shasta. Clustering around the roaring fires Gary made, we cooked, sang, and slept under the stars. Altogether it was wonderfully memorable.

During this time, Nancy and Gary and Nina and Paul had been building their lives in Southern California not too far away from us. Every chance they got, they visited us with their active little ones. Each grandchild was a blessing and more reason for joy.

There was much for the children to do where we lived. We loved it that our home was such a great place for the grandkids and that our children could share so much of their lives with us. Bob spent hours teaching the grands to swim in our pool. Having the young ones racing everywhere, full of chatter and new discoveries, was unbelievably delightful for us.

And finally Bob became a powerboat owner—something he had longed for. He bought a Skipjack 20 and docked it in the Back Bay. We could think of no better name for her than *Mekong Mama*. We joined the Bahia Corinthian Yacht Club close by. The kids could now indulge in every sort of water sport, including ocean water-skiing. Endless hours were spent together cruising Balboa Bay and sometimes going to Catalina Island.

This picture of Bob shows Catalina's casino in the background.

Being back in California naturally linked our lives again with Nolan and Mary and their family. Nolan had maintained his optometry practice with an office close by, but he also had become involved in politics and had held a number of public offices. It was fun to be a part of supporting him as he campaigned for his elections.

Mary and Nolan, with their three stunning sons and beautiful daughter, made an outstandingly attractive family.

People were naturally magnetized to Nolan. I believe his family had a great deal to do with that. However, Nolan's dedication to politics took a heavy toll. Mary began to hate the demands of that life, and their personal problems grew. This led to a bitter divorce that struck us all tragically. Bob and I stood by them both, but Mary and the children were estranged from Nolan.

When he was running for the California State Assembly, his team organized a huge rally on the lawn of a scenic park in Fountain Valley. The bleachers were packed with noisy, flag-waving supporters, and we were the noisiest.

As drums rolled, an official helicopter landed at a designated clearing, and Governor Ronald Reagan stepped out, his hands raised high in greeting. Nolan and others greeted him warmly and led him to the podium, where he gave a glowing speech in support of Nolan. After refreshments and handshakes all around, Reagan returned to his waiting helicopter to fly back to Sacramento. Good friends are there for each other.

The big night of the final vote tally for his race for state assemblyman was held at the Costa Mesa Marriott Hotel. We were all gathered in the crowded penthouse rooms, listening and watching the results of the voting as they came across on TV monitors. At dawn the final tally was in. Nolan won! What whoops and hollers! As the sun came up, Bob and I departed for home, deeply touched and proud of Nolan's kids who had all turned out to share their Dad's victory. Nolan served in the California assembly from 1980 to 1992.

One of Nolan's faithful workers was Ina Evans. After dating for four years, they were married in a gorgeous garden belonging to close friends, followed by a lively reception. Nolan's attendants were Bob and Morrill, our step brother.

Their marriage was the start of thirty-three years of devotion to each other. Ina has continued to be a precious and interested supporter for us all.

Meanwhile, Bob continued his commute to LAX and his work there. The years slipped by happily with their procession of birthdays, Christmases, and everything in between.

Over these years, Bob was very active in the 5th Marine Division Association of Retirees. Their annual reunion was held in a different state each year, depending on where the organizing host lived. In 1976 Bob volunteered to host the event in California. We chose the famous hotel at Universal Studios as the venue. He and I spent months planning it. For the entire week beforehand we were at the hotel itself, busy with reservations and preparations. It was quite a large affair, culminating in a formal banquet.

At the banquet, special guests were scattered throughout the room among the retired marines and their families at patriotically decorated tables. Bob and I were seated at the upper tier of the four-tiered dais, between the general of Camp Pendleton and his wife. Also on the dais was Joe Rosenthal. Joe's iconic photograph of the flag raising at Iwo Jima has become a tribute to the victory and was the inspiration for the Iwo Jima Monument in Arlington, Virginia.

Seeing Joe Rosenthal that night brought Bob's conversation about Iwo Jima back to me vividly. I remembered being curled up with him on the couch at Mother's home after the war as he revealed to me his war experiences. I could see the action replayed again, just as I had pictured it when Bob described it to me many years before.

The 5th Division was part of the invading forces that took Iwo Jima. In preparation for the launching of the landing boats, Bob was assigned to the underwater reconnaissance team of two hundred frogmen. They were dropped off from small boats to swim and dive down to survey the bottom of the ocean to be sure that there were no mines to obstruct the landing boats in the invasion. Then the underwater crews were to return to the transport ship and report their findings, their mission accomplished.

But when Bob got back to the ship, as soon as he made his report to the commanding officer, he jumped into the very first landing craft as it left the ship headed for the beach— with no rifle.

"But you're always supposed to take your rifle!" I gasped.

He explained that everything happened so fast there hadn't been a moment to spare. They were under heavy mortar fire from caves on the mountain, and our ships were blasting from the sea. There were immediate casualties on landing, so he grabbed a rifle from a marine who had been killed and then proceeded up the beach.

They slithered up, foot by foot, capturing the land by slowly scrambling their way up Mount Suribachi. Bob said that when he was halfway up the hill, he looked up to see his fellow marines raising the first American flag. Everybody cheered. Then a command was given to go back to the ship for a bigger flag, more reflective of the huge victory.

In a post-war interview, Joe was modest when asked about taking that picture. He had been a news photographer and said he "just happened to catch the flag-raising out of the corner of his eye." Instinctively he swung his camera around and shot blindly. His famous shot was of the second flag.

Bob, handsome in his white dinner jacket and ready to open the banquet's final ceremonies, rose from his seat next to me. The room silenced. Then in a loud, commanding voice he addressed the honor guard who stood at attention in their formal finery at the back of the room.

"Gentlemen, present arms!"

Instantly they raised their rifles. Then in crisp cadence, flag bearers leading, they marched in double file down the center aisle directly toward us, parting precisely when they reached the dais to march off to either side of the room. The fine traditions of the corps were reflected by the honor and respect shown by these disciplined young marines.

That moment was a huge, meaningful thrill to Bob. It was very moving, and I was exceedingly privileged to have been a part of that reunion of brave and worthy men.

There began to be some talk in the office that there would probably be a need for Bob to go to Bangkok again for Continental and that it might not be short-term. Instead of the way we had approached previous tours, with Bob going ahead and leaving me to follow after closing things up, we decided that this time we would leave together. That meant we needed to prepare in advance. Reluctantly we sold our Irvine Terrace home and moved to a temporary apartment in Corona del Mar that overlooked the ocean and parkways.

However, the possible overseas assignment was not materializing. One day, while going for a drive, we ran across a real estate drawing for unbuilt condos on the Mission Viejo Country Club Golf Course. Due to the housing shortage, these drawings were popular. For a laugh, we entered our name, and it turned out were one of the winners. Of course, we had to wait till it was built and the area developed, but time passed quickly. Before we knew it, we moved and were glad for the new home, still close enough to continue our boating and playing in Balboa and Newport.

Unfortunately, the news from overseas was growing steadily more grim.

> On April 30, 1975, Communist North Vietnamese and Viet Cong forces captured the South Vietnamese capital of Saigon, forcing South Vietnam to surrender and bringing about an end to the Vietnam War. . . . In the weeks leading up to the fall of Saigon, the United States organized the evacuation of Americans and South Vietnamese orphans and refugees from the city. On April 29 and 30, the United States frantically rescued all remaining Americans and some Vietnamese via helicopter. . . . However, thousands

of South Vietnamese desperate to escape were left
stranded outside the embassy.

—*From Associated Press article in the New York Times,*
May 1, 1975

From our condo in Mission Viejo, we watched the
news, aghast as Continental's aircraft heroically flew the
final rescue missions of friends and allies from the rooftop
of the Saigon embassy and from the airfield. The images
of people climbing up on one another to be jammed into
the helicopters while under fire are indelible and became
symbols of the Vietnam War. Such a frantic time. For us it
was a crushing moment.

As had been predicted by many, there followed the
inevitable domino effect, which pulled down Laos and
Cambodia. Our courageous Hmong friends now faced not
only the loss of their country's freedom but also the loss of
their home country as it had been. In spite of our mutual
effort to keep the communist Pathet Lao from overrunning
Laos, the faithful Hmong people were defeated and run out
of their country. The capital and the entire country were
devastated.

The United States went to valiant efforts to evacuate the
Hmong to Thai refugee camps and helped those who sought
a new life in America with means to get there and restart
their lives. Tragically the people who could not escape
to America or refugee camps were tortured, killed, and
stripped of all possessions by the communists. It is terribly
sad and disheartening to hear of their struggles since 1975.

Part of the consequences of the losses in Laos was that all American businesses in that region closed. Bob was asked by Six to return to Bangkok to oversee the selling of ninety aircraft no longer needed in Vientiane and Bangkok. While there for three months, Bob also found work for the many indigenous employees who had been faithful workers over the years.

It was then that Bob and I took on a personal mission of our own. We both felt compelled to offer sponsorship to our loyal Thai and Vietnamese friends and their families. As a result we were able to secure for two families (a total of twenty people) legal entrance into the United States. These people were extraordinary and brave.

They later became naturalized citizens in a very moving ceremony in the Los Angeles Coliseum, with many others who had been welcomed into this country after the Vietnam War. We were there with them as they raised their right hands and pledged their allegiance to the United States of America. They were profoundly grateful and keenly aware of the privilege of becoming US citizens. I doubt anyone left the stadium that day dry-eyed.

Bob decided it was time to retire from Continental. It was nice to think of him no longer having to make that daily commute to Los Angeles. We were exploring what more leisurely days would look like.

He had been retired all of three full days when suddenly, on the fourth morning, in came a game-changing phone call. I had been out at the time, doing what we called the green belt committee check of our condo property. When I came back, he was trying hard to read the paper, but I saw excitement lighting up his face. He couldn't hold it in.

"Guess what?"

Pregnant pause.

"Six called and it took me all of thirteen seconds to say yes! We're off to Taipei!"

I gulped, thinking to myself, *What about me? Do I have a say in this?*

But knowing Bob, he was already restless. He was not cut out for retirement. I knew there was nothing I could do but join him.

Why Taiwan? The answer to that question lies in post-World War II history. The Chinese government, exiled to Taiwan, was led by Chiang Kai-shek for twenty-five years following Mao's takeover of mainland China.

> This government [in Taiwan] continued to be recognised by many countries as the legitimate government of China, and Taiwan controlled China's seat in the United Nations until the end of Chiang's life. He died on 5 April 1975.
>
> —*BBC History*

While our time in Taipei was after Chiang himself had passed away, his legacy was palpable there and the grief still deep among the people.

America supported Chiang's government in exile, hoping to see the eventual overturn of communism on the mainland. Madame Chiang, his US-educated wife, was his advocate with the West. The pro-West government in Taiwan welcomed American businesses to locate there.

Bob Six had been monitoring Taiwan carefully, with an eye on air service in and out of Taipei. However, in 1979, circumstances stateside were uncertain. President Jimmy Carter announced the United States was no longer going to support the government of Taiwan. Yet here was an American company, CAL, about to establish business there. It was an awkward position.

In spite of the signals from Washington, Six encouraged both of us to go on Continental's behalf to set up the Taipei office. His thought was that the two of us together would help create an atmosphere of permanence and stability. We took that in a broader sense to mean not only the permanence and stability of Continental but also our personal opportunity, as Americans, to communicate support for the efforts toward democracy being made in Taiwan.

So we went ahead as planned, assuring the local business community that we were enthusiastic and ready to work among them. At first we stayed at the palatial Imperial Hotel. We had a corner suite with a breathtaking view overlooking the city, air conditioning, and a convenient little kitchen arrangement. Just ideal. The hotel had ample facilities. We could easily invite local dignitaries and embassy people, making relevant connections for the work at hand.

Living at the Imperial would have suited me just fine for the duration; however, besides setting up an office in Taipei, Bob was expected to also establish an official residence for the company. In the Yangmingshan Hills there was a small international community where many of the people from the various embassies lived. Bob leased a spacious French Colonial house there, thinking I would like it. It even had a swimming pool (which we never used).

But at 1,500 feet above the city, the weather was frigid with strong winds that January. The house was a high-ceilinged barn of a place, way past its prime, drafty and cold, with black and white square marble floors. I stopped still on my initial walk-through, alarmed by the damp mold on the library walls that would have to be scraped off—hopefully.

Bob said to me sweetly, "I know you can transform this place."

I heard myself say, "Okay," as my mind tried to grasp the countless challenges to be overcome. Although I had no clue of how or where to start, I came up with a plan and stuck to it.

Luckily I was able to employ a good housekeeper (amah) who was capable of the work to clean up the place, and she also did the cooking. Her name was Ahco; she was a pretty young woman, very happy to be working with us. I would get her started in the morning and then taxi into the city to store-hop.

First, I was on a mission to get the bare essentials. The list of brooms, mops, pails, kitchen utensils, linens, and you name it trailed off the page. Next, I searched amid the stalls and small shops for the most appealing and fitting furnishings, drapes, and accessories. Along the way I would communicate the best I could with the shopkeepers and learn who could be hired to help with the small jobs of installation and transporting purchases.

I became a part of the bustling Chinese city. It was enchanting and charming; the people were cheerful and warm. Also I began to get a real sense of the Chinese culture. There was a magnificent museum that the General and Madame Chiang had established for the viewing of the priceless treasures they had managed to salvage from the mainland. They had known full well Mao Tse-tung's total disrespect for China's antiquities. The transported treasures were stored in caves in the mountains. The museum displayed revolving exhibits of those stored items. The artistry was almost heart-stopping. One huge, intricately carved ivory temple replica was so awesomely exquisite that I teared openly as I stood before it. We toured the museum when we could, always urging visitors not to miss it.

Madame Chiang (Soong Mei-ling), in particular, intrigued me. I quote from a CBS news article about her after her death at the age of 106 in her New York home in 2003:

> Madame Chiang and Chiang Kai-shek were one of the world's most famous couples. They married in 1926, a year after Mr. Chiang, also known as the Generalissimo, took over China's ruling Nationalist Party. . . . Though born in the East, Madame Chiang was thoroughly Western in thought and philosophy. Brought up in a Methodist family, she studied in America from the age of 10 to 19 and graduated with honors from Wellesley College in Massachusetts in 1917.
>
> "The only thing Oriental about me is my face," she once said. Her supporters said she was a powerful force for international friendship, understanding and good.
>
> —*CBS/Associated Press release, October 24, 2003*

My days of work bringing our little mansion to life were interspersed with trips home every two or three weeks, thoughtfully arranged by Bob. Those few days were marvelous and just enough time to check on things at our condo, see the girls, and enjoy home for a change.

The travel part was a breeze with our airline privileges. I could just appear and get on a first-class flight. Sometimes my layover would be in Japan and other times in Hawaii. You may wonder about the effects of jet leg. Not bad really—I was much younger then.

But once back at the Taipei residence, the cold dampness of the place engulfed me. Each morning the marble floors would have to be mopped to remove the moisture that beaded on top like dew, without the sun to redeem it. The library, which had startled me on the initial walk-through, never did recover from its mildew.

I would shiver and tote around my little portable radio from room to room. There was one US forces overseas station that reached Taipei. It was the only English-speaking station and my link with the world. Yet, as much as I tried, I couldn't shake my unprecedented bouts of loneliness. That wasn't like me, and it was unnerving. Nightmares woke me frequently, and I'd find myself all weepy.

Bob was aware of my sadness. We were about six months into the stint, and as we talked, we began to see that the initial goal to set up things in Taipei was essentially accomplished. He had made a viable office, and there was now a substantial and comfortable home for Continental's Taipei manager. In fact, we had already been able to host some small dinner parties there, in addition to the larger affairs at the Imperial. It was known that the French Colonial home high in the Yangmingshan Hills was Continental's residence. That being the case, Bob managed to exchange jobs with a colleague in the LA Continental office. The new manager would be able to slip into place behind Bob easily.

Soon we were back in our familiar condo in Mission Viejo.

When he transferred back to Continental in Los Angeles, Bob was certain that he wanted to move on. As much as he had thrived in his career with Continental, he was ready for a new challenge on a different scale. He made this retirement from CAL permanent.

Immediately Bob then joined with close friends to partner in a new company called Group Systems International. GSI's aim was to establish offices in distant cities to represent airlines where they had no presence. Obviously this was a venture for which Bob's experience had completely prepared him—yet it would not be for long.

He was in his office with his partner, Fritz, and on the phone with another partner, Clyde, in Japan when he had sudden, fatal heart failure. It was June 11, 1981. He was sixty, and I was fifty-seven.

I was waiting for Bob to come home to dinner when Fritz called me, sobbing. I wanted to be at Bob's side more than anything and cried out, "I'll be right there!" But Fritz told me there was no point. Because Bob had died in the office, there would have to be an autopsy, and his body was being taken away. He said that everything that could be done had been done—CPR, paramedics, everything. His death had been instant.

The night turned ever more tragic and surreal for me because I could not find where Bob's body had been taken. I made many calls to morgues, mortuaries, anywhere I could think of, to no avail. It was all I could see to do. Of course, I was in shock.

Then there were the countless calls to family and friends. Everyone else was in shock. Finally his body was taken to Pacific View Mortuary the following morning, where I stayed by his side, holding his still hand.

The suddenness of his dying so young was indescribably terrible for me. And not just for me and not just for the girls; there were many, many people, near and far, powerfully affected by his unexpected death. The unity of our shared sorrow somehow blunted the pain for me. I was numb. That numbness over the initial days helped immeasurably. Now I see death differently—certainly my own. But I am talking of then and the agony of a woman who has just lost half of herself.

*How fast the tide sweeps in, and all our sandcastles
float away . . .*

His funeral was at Pacific View in Corona del Mar. On the night before the service, a few of us were in the chapel, getting it prepared. The casket was already in place and open. Bob looked so alive—with even a slight smile on his face. No formal wake was planned, but a spontaneous one transpired that night.

Sam, the attendant up in the sound booth, was setting up the music to be played during the service. Nolan was by Bob's side, straightening his tie and fussing over him.

Some close friends and family gathered around us, recalling stories about Bob, encompassing everything from mischief to heroism. When the memories brought tears, my friend Claire, who lived close by, took charge.

"Enough! What are we crying for? Bob would call for a celebration. We're all together!" She left and quickly returned with welcomed lively refreshments.

Raising our glasses, someone called out to the sound booth for Bob's favorite song, "My Way," sung by Frank Sinatra. The recurring line about doing it *my way* had been Bob's motto for life. As we recalled more and more great stories, the request went up repeatedly to the sound booth, "Play it again, Sam!"

Nothing could have been better for me that night than the intimate, warm, compassionate love of caring friends and family.

These details express to you who I was then. There would be much more for me to learn in time. For one thing, when I sing that song now, I change the words to apply to me. More than anything else, my heartfelt prayer is that I do things God's way, not mine.

The next day dawned with an agenda that my mind could scarcely fathom. I would be going to Bob's funeral.

The chapel was packed to overflowing, with chairs constantly being added outside. My head spun as I tried to take in the faces from the various stages of his life. I could see Clyde, who on such short notice had caught a flight from Tokyo. There was no limit to family, of course, plus personal and business friends, military friends, Vietnamese, Chinese, and Thai friends.

His outstanding service record was honored by a flag-draped casket, "Taps," and military salute. What a great privilege it was for me and my family to have the young honor guard fold the flag covering Bob's casket and ceremoniously hand it to Colonel Bill Barber, who then presented it to me. This tribute touched me deeply.

Bill Barber had been a dear and close Marine Corps friend of Bob's since Guadalcanal/Iwo Jima days and, more recently, had looked forward to their times together at the yearly 5th Marine reunions. He was the recipient of the Purple Heart, Silver Star, and Medal of Honor awards, and he had spent his entire career in active military service. He was a humble man. And, unbeknownst to me, he had been the one to arrange for Bob's military ceremony.

And the flowers! I love flowers and always notice them. But I can honestly say I don't think I have ever seen more in one place than on that Sunday in June.

As the ceremony drew to a close, it was announced that there would be no graveside service, since Bob would be cremated and his ashes placed in the mortuary's Valencia Court. I couldn't help noticing that over to the side Bob's two elderly aunts were visibly upset, showing clear disapproval of something. Inquiring why, I learned that according to their tradition, it was customary for the casket to be open so that the relatives of the deceased could be sure that the right body was in there. As absurd as it seemed to the mortuary attendants, I asked if they would kindly arrange to escort the aunts to the casket privately for a consoling check inside. All was well.

Making the event complete was our unforgettably caring Iranian neighbor, who had only recently come to the United

States. She and other neighbors generously took care of all the refreshments for the reception held at our home. The mortuary transported all the flowers to the condo. For weeks I was clipping and rearranging the flowers, letting each one remind me of something special to cherish about my Bob and each bouquet speak to me of the incredibly kind people giving me much needed solace.

On the following Thursday, I was leaving San Diego, where I had been visiting Nina. As I drove up Highway 1, a horrible feeling engulfed my whole body, so much so that I had to pull over to the side, where I wept and wept. Finally I recovered sufficiently to finish the drive. Arriving home, I called the mortuary and was updated with the fact that Bob's body had been cremated at exactly the time when I had to pull over the car.

Soul ties.

Later it occurred to me to do something that would both please Nolan and honor Bob. I lent the huge flag from Bob's ceremony to Nolan, knowing how much it would mean to him. He hung it prominently in his headquarters, and it was there during all the rest of his re-election campaigns for the California State Assembly. He would never forget his best friend and the service he had given for his country. They were both true patriots.

Then several years after Bob's death, there seemed a need for us as a family to further honor his memory. Nina, Nancy, Debby, and I brainstormed ideas and concluded we'd start a traditional picnic over the Memorial Day weekend to remember him and all others in our family who had served our country. It has grown in both size and meaning and now includes the families of cousins, nieces, and nephews. It is a close-knit group of caring, fun-loving, smart adults. Grands and great-grands abound.

The host of loved ones who have now departed are still with us in memory. I'm grateful that the Memorial Weekend tradition continues. Now there's even a second extended-family tradition—a fun summer campout every year.

Chapter 8

LIVING WATER

Awakening

*1*982—the year after Bob died. What do you do when the bottom falls out of your world? I guess it really depends on each individual. Being a resilient woman, I soon coaxed myself to get on with life. I thought about dropping out for a while but instead chose to get involved and busy. But something was wrong. I had to admit it was all motions really, just empty motions. Without my traveling partner to follow, I craved a compass.

At that critical time, feeling quite lost at sea, Gordon Swayze, my optometrist, asked me a casual question while I sat in his examining chair. "Do you have a Bible at home, Sue?"

I quipped lightly, "Sure. On my bookshelf!"

My glib answer to Gordon gave him all the information he needed to press on further. He knew my feelings of being lost without Bob, but he also discerned I was lost in the sense of needing the presence of the Savior in my life.

That simple exchange began a pathway of awakening and learning for me, a process of growing that has continued ever more exciting to this day. I was to learn there is an immense difference between intellectually acknowledging the presence of God and getting to know him in an interactive, one-on-one relationship. It is one thing to believe *about* Jesus and quite another to believe *in* him.

Over the next six months Gordon truly discipled me. It could easily have been two thousand years before. Jesus became alive in my heart as well as in my brain. We pored over his holy Word, with books and papers spread everywhere on my dining room table. We delved deeply into the great books of the Old Testament—the historical books, the wisdom books of Psalms and Proverbs, and the books of the Prophets. Then we delved into the New Testament with the words of Jesus himself in the Gospels, the letters by some of his apostles, and the final prophesies of Revelation. God's awesome plan of redemption was illumined as mercy and faith revealed what had previously been hidden from my eyes.

We attended Chuck Smith's Calvary Chapel in Costa Mesa, where Gordon had been Chuck's Bible student. Gordon and I talked earnestly and frequently by phone as he led me through studies and addressed my endless questions and doubts.

One of the first assignments he gave me was to list on a lined pad every sin I had ever committed. While I intellectually accepted that I had come from a background of mortal mind, I was not aware of personal guilt for any sin, much less for some awful kind of sin. I had not been taught that sin is sin—whether great or small.

Although I had been a Christian from childhood, active in Sunday schools and choirs, I began to understand why my belief was not enough to fill the void in me. My faith had been a form of faith by works. And truth be told, Bob had filled my heart so fully that I had not previously been aware of God's rightful place of supremacy.

Gordon and I discussed the philosophy of "good enough," referring to the common notion that heaven is a default reward for doing the right things. Then a verse from Matthew struck me like lightning: "Not everyone who says to me, 'Lord, Lord,' shall enter the kingdom of heaven." Gradually, gently, respectfully, and lovingly the Holy Spirit began to open my heart to the God of relationship, revealing his endless love for me so I could love him back with my whole heart—not my Sunday-best, dressed-up heart.

Without condemnation, yet with a conviction of my own unworthiness, I started to make my list. It filled two whole lined pages. I was flabbergasted. There was an abundance of small yet harmful things like feelings of pride, critical and judgmental attitudes, and even self-deprecation—more than enough to pollute my heart and set it in direct conflict with God's Word. It greatly saddened me.

Then Gordon said, "If you are ready, ask God for his divine forgiveness and invite Jesus to dwell in you through the presence of his Holy Spirit."

I prayed, and Gordon agreed with me in that prayer.

Then he said dramatically, "Now rip up the pages and throw them away!"

All I had been taught suddenly hit me as real. I realized that when we humble ourselves before God, acknowledging our unworthiness in light of his awesome, unfathomable holiness and love for us, he not only forgives us, he also forgets.

My burden of past stupid actions was utterly washed away. I knew without any doubt the truth that Jesus had paid the ransom for me and all who call on his holy name. He was God's son made man on this earth, a historic figure, who taught us of the kingdom of God, promised us eternal life, then suffered and died. He rose again to prove that he *is*, indeed, the promised Messiah, the Son of God, and to give us hope for our eternal future together with him.

Before his death, Jesus promised his distraught disciples that he would never leave them nor forsake them; that he would send the Holy Spirit to dwell within each one who believes in him. I now know that we have that same power within us, to help, instruct, comfort, protect, show us the way, and give us the words when we don't have the words to pray.

John 17 perfectly explains the indwelling Spirit. We are one with God the Father and with God the Son, through the Holy Spirit who dwells within us when we accept Jesus as our Lord. That is rebirth in the Spirit, sometimes called the Baptism of the Holy Spirit, and sometimes referred to as being "born again." I have experienced this and continue to experience it. This new life in the Spirit is my prayer for you.

I cried out from deep in my soul the special word used in worship, "Hallelujah!" Translation—"Praise the Lord!" A sense of excitement, gratitude, devotion, and overwhelming joy swept over this follower of Christ Jesus.

Soon after that, Gordon prodded, "Sue, you do know, don't you, that you're going to have to leave that positive-thinking-theology church?"

I knew he referred to Robert Schuller, Jr.'s church in Capistrano which I had been attending. That church had been founded by his father and now has been carried forward by the third generation, the grandson, who goes by the name Bobby. I salute young Bobby's church, Shepherd's Grove, for it is truly Spirit-filled, and he is greatly inspired. But back then, it was his father's church. I had become their wedding coordinator, a job that offered me vicarious beauty, love, and happiness. I had been attracted to that atmosphere because I felt it would fill the emptiness in my heart after losing my precious Bob.

Gordon's remark about leaving the church caught me up short. After a few moments of silent reflection and a deep breath, however, I opened my eyes to their widest and looked directly at him. "You know what?" I asked, pausing for emphasis. "I get it!"

Then we both put our heads back and laughed long, luxuriating in the peace.

That day was the start of my making decisions with my new set of priorities. I had knowingly and purposefully switched allegiance in my heart from the earthly kingdom of this seen world to the unseen kingdom of God. Jesus was now my Lord, and I would never again look at anything the same way. I had a new standard: to love God above all and to allow every day to be shaped by his purpose for my life.

The motto of my girlhood, "Remember who you are and who you represent," gained its ultimate perspective. I am a child of the King of the universe, "an ambassador for

Christ," as Paul teaches in 2 Corinthians 5:20. How can pride in family prestige, school, ambition, success, or any other ideal take precedence? Whatever I have or do is all by the grace, mercy, and the gifts that he has given.

It is pretty simple really. Through Jesus, entire lives are transformed. Sadly, we have been restricted from saying—because of political correctness—that Jesus is the only way. He said of himself, "I am the way, the truth, and the life. No one comes to the Father except through me" (John 14:6).

There was another profound truth that Gordon helped me to grasp—grace. We can never earn nor can we deserve God's forgiveness, his love, his gift of eternal life, or his Holy Spirit in us. We are *all* imperfect. God's unmerited favor of grace is the key we must hold. Through his grace to us, we can look with compassion on even the most unlovable human beings, loving them with the heart of Christ. This is the *living water* of his Holy Spirit flowing freely through us.

Soon Gordon's work caused him to relocate out of the area, but I took his advice and not long afterward was fortunate to find a nondenominational community church in Dana Point that was powerful. I was baptized with fourteen other believers in the harbor there at a small private beach. Other church members gathered on the sand to witness and celebrate with us. The formal rite of baptism, together with continuing Bible studies, firmly set me on a course of solid commitment to our Lord and Savior.

One series on biblical doctrine and prophesy I attended was led by a prominent Christian speaker, Walter Martin. He was a scholarly and distinguished apologist and author. I went to all the sessions, taking special note of one in which he stressed the power of evil, which can attach itself to objects—in particular, objects of worship to false gods and idols. Living in an atmosphere with such statues or pictures is an invitation to spirits of darkness.

During our years in Asia I had collected many religious icons, innocently viewing them purely as works of art. Some were astonishingly beautiful and intricate in their workmanship. So one foggy night, when the teaching was over, I asked Walter to come out to my car to help me to know which artifacts I should remove from my home. With the help of a flashlight, we sorted through the boxes of questionable items in the trunk of my car. Patiently and prayerfully, he weeded out the idols. I was grateful to him, as the knowledge of their danger had been a burden to me.

But then, a new problem: I was reluctant even to return home with them. Driving through the ghostly fog, I sought a dumpster, but all the close ones had forbidding warnings: "Private! No Dumping!" Finally I found a legal one and deposited Buddha replicas that had been designed for worship. "No other gods before me" (Exodus 20:3) can be many things in this day and age—lifestyle, people, and even theologies.

I must share two miracles that I was blessed with early in my walk with Christ. There have been subsequent ones, but these were early and helped me, as they were true signs of his work in me, strengthening my new faith in his presence and his personal care for me.

The first had to do with the fact that for years I had been a smoker. I prayed, asking God to take away the habit and cravings I felt. Within one week, I had absolutely no desire to smoke. And now I am more fully appreciating the extent of the healing from that addiction as I see many residents where I now live with their ever-present canisters of oxygen.

The second miracle concerned the unreasonable fears that invaded me after Bob's death. Previously fear had not been a lingering issue for me, although certainly I had been in a few situations when I experienced raw fear. But those were times when there had been a palpable enemy. So it was unnerving for me when I began to have serious yet unwarranted fears that disturbed my spirit so much that sleep was difficult without chairs propped under door handles. My ears were attuned to the slightest noises, each signaling the threat of invasion. Again I prayed earnestly, asking for deliverance. Again, within only one week, I was free.

My newfound life with the Lord imbued me with a sense of peace. I was able to adjust to my life without Bob and felt confident within my faith—so much so, I lost sight of the second part of the equation. There is good and there is the antithesis of good. We have an enemy of our souls, called Satan, who searches the world "like a roaring lion, seeking whom he may devour," as the Bible warns in 1 Peter 5:8. I had let my guard down, forgetting the power of that enemy.

People who are mature in the Lord will tell you readily that after a mountaintop experience, such as my coming to know Christ personally, the old devil crashes in and tries to control. I had become vulnerable and began making bad judgments. I had certainly prayed for wisdom and discernment, but that fell short when my self-will got in the way. In 1984 I thought I was in love to the point of marriage.

Hank was an acquaintance of Nolan's from his campaign for the California State Assembly. He was witty, played bridge as I did, and we got along wonderfully as we dated.

I told my pastor and sought his blessings. No! He insisted we must first have counseling. At my age? Hardly. I thought I knew it all. Hank was Catholic, and so we asked his priest. Again, no! We must first have counseling.

Undaunted, he and I obstinately went to the justice of the peace in Santa Ana and were married shortly before Christmas. When the family gathered at my condo for Christmas Eve, they saw our announcement of marriage and license on the coffee table on a flowered platter. They seemed glad for us as we celebrated with a family banquet at an elegant restaurant in Laguna Beach.

Since Hank and I both liked Redlands where Nancy and Gary lived, we decided to settle there too and bought a lovely home in the Smiley Heights area. Hank did a meticulous job of moving us. It was springtime, fragrant orange-blossom time, and our garden continually surprised us with new blooms. Must be heaven.

Wrong.

I soon discovered that Hank had a horrible temper with sustained bouts of rage. Living with him became a living nightmare. I choose to recount it here only to point out the importance (and biblically, it is true) of being yoked to a person of complete spiritual compatibility and understanding. We were poles apart in that arena as well as everything else. No amount of reasoning worked.

The eleven months I spent with him were eleven months of verbal abuse, no financial support, and social isolation—except for family. Worst of all, a frightening change in my character was taking place. I had no idea that I was capable of the anger that arose in me, fired by a sense of justice. I was determined not to let myself be changed.

On a spiritual level, I felt that I was fighting with the devil himself, who wanted to claim me for his own. I hated everything about what was happening, dug in my heels, and with a strength that came straight from the Lord, I demanded that he leave. He did so, and was out of my life, moving to live with his mother in Sedona.

We got a divorce—an annulment really—for ours had been a mockery of a marriage.

I had learned a hard lesson.

> *Lord, thank you that I could come to you, and you gave me the grace of your forgiveness and your mercy. You loved me no less and I loved you even more.*

Chapter 9

CALIFORNIA DESERT REDLANDS

Serenity

One beautiful day in Redlands, I woke early with a mission in mind. I drove to Palm Springs to buy a rosebush root at the big nursery there and have it delivered and planted for my close friend, Betty, from Newport days. She had recently lost her mother, Rosie, who was also my friend.

The day was sparkling, and I felt exhilarated and free after the traumatic events of Hank. The rose gift selection complete, I began to take in more of the surrounding desert beauty. I was positively euphoric. Spotting a Century 21 Real Estate office, I entered without hesitation and inquired about condos.

A cheerful real estate agent drove me around to my enthusiastic oohs and aahs. In no time, I was thoroughly enchanted by a condo in Palm Desert, up Highway 74. The imposing, lighted cross standing on the hill nearby seemed prophetic and beckoning. That same afternoon, I bought the bougainvillea-covered condo and happily drove back to Redlands to announce my new home to Nancy.

"You did what?"

The Redlands house sold quickly, and I made a good profit. I then downsized and launched eagerly toward whatever might lie ahead for me. One thing was certain, I was ready to change gears and leave my recent past in the dust.

The Christmas holidays were fast-approaching when I moved to Palm Desert. Much work had to be done on the new place. In the local newspaper, I discovered an ad by a young couple, just married, who needed a job immediately. The three of us dug in side by side—cleaning, wallpapering, and painting. By New Year's Eve, tired but satisfied, my two young coworkers and I celebrated my new desert home.

Marge and Charlie, a couple who lived down the greenbelt slope from me, kindly invited me to join their home Bible study. The three of us soon became close friends. And more, there was a women's study group that gathered for a monthly breakfast at Coco's.

Enticing things to do popped up continually. The one I especially looked forward to was volunteering at the new McCallum Theater. I was one of their ushers, dressed for the part in a smart gray jacket and dark blue skirt. As such, I saw their varied, excellent productions free of charge.

I became involved in a number of other meaningful groups, like Southwest Community Church and the Forest Home Women's Auxiliary. Also, since I was now living in proximity to Betty, she and I could spend more time together. More often than not, something would click, bringing up past shenanigans and sending us rolling with laughter. That naturally led to creating some fresh escapades to add to the list.

When a gentlemanly neighbor, Art, offered to show me the well-known spots around town, I was flattered but a bit flustered. He came on the scene soon after my arrival, when the idea of being shown around was appealing. I accepted his offers of local tours and nice dinners. Yet naggingly I knew this relationship was something I needed to present in prayer; however, when I did, I got no sense of guidance. I took silence as tacit agreement and proceeded on my own— even as red flags began to proliferate. Being naive (a common failing of single women, I fear), I kept attributing the best of intentions to his attentions.

Finally—thankfully—I went to the Lord again, this time genuinely seeking his lead. It reassures and somehow amuses me that God is the keenest discerner of my heart. It is impossible to be fake with him. He sees all, knows all, and knows me better than I know myself. Being open before him and sensing his will in this, I finally faced myself in the mirror and lectured my reflection: *Sue, you are really losing it. Remember how God intricately worked out his perfect plan for you with Bob? Remember where stubborn self-will got you with Hank? All you need is another fiasco.*

My words to myself were hard stones; the Holy Spirit's words inside were gentle and forgiving. As I yielded to him, my temptations were harnessed with God's perfect protection; my bearings were back; my anchor was firm. I stopped seeing Art. God would provide his choice for me in his timing.

I began to learn for myself that the desert is, indeed, a perfect teaching field. It's no wonder there are many examples of God's leading his people into the desert to sharpen them. There is something magical and awesome about the stark beauty of the starry skies, the rich hews of sunsets, the warm and pure air, and the carved-out mountain ridges. One cannot help but be overcome by the grandeur of God's creation there—day and night. I bowed in deep humbleness to his majesty. I believe it was this glory displayed dramatically before me that caused me to really pay very close attention to what the Creator himself was trying to communicate to me.

Even today I am mystified by how I could have lived nearly sixty years with blinders on—not knowing this wondrous God. How could I have lived so long, had so many experiences, met so many people, been in so many countries, and yet not known Him? But then I turn that around to say,

Thank you, Lord, that you made yourself real to me
in time for me to have years more to get to know you.

I love to share the next part of the story.

For some time, everyone in our prayer group had been joining me in prayer for a dedicated Christian man to come into my life. It happened that Jim Catalano, a recent widower, drove out to the desert from San Diego to visit Marge and

Charlie. He was actually a relative of theirs. They introduced me to Jim one morning at Coco's. What I didn't know at the time was that Marge and Charlie had also been saying the same prayer for him: to find a godly wife.

There was an unmistakable chemistry between us that day we were introduced. Neither one of us wanted to say goodbye abruptly after breakfast, so I ventured to ask him if he would like me to show him some of the beauty of the desert before his return to San Diego. Delighted, he accepted.

We spent the entire day together, talking nonstop as we took in one stunning vista after the next. After a delicious dinner, while we sat together in the elegant lobby of the Marriott Desert Springs Hotel, he asked me to marry him. In my mind's eye, I see us sitting together, like part of the desert's magical night view. We were both as sure as we could be even on that first day that we were each God's answer to the other's separate prayers.

As though our spiritual bonding wasn't enough, God added the bonuses that he was a dashingly handsome Italian and funny as well as fun loving. Though he was eighty-one, he looked for all the world to be a youthful sixty-five. I was seventy, so the age match was just fine.

My girls were generous in their acceptance of Jim. His two boys were the same of me; however, his only daughter, Marilyn, found the idea more difficult to accept. I understood, since this was relatively soon after her mother's death. However, Jim was resolute. He believed our senior status meant our time was short, so we should not let her reluctance stop the marriage.

Two months after our introduction, Jim and I were married in San Diego. I have a frame on my wall with a collection of pictures from that day. It includes a copy of the words he and I wrote together for the ceremony. Those lines perfectly capture our feelings for each other and reflect how tightly bound we were in God's love.

Since Jim enjoyed the desert too, we agreed he would move into my place in Rancho Mirage, where I had relocated not long before meeting him. We needed nothing else now except the continued presence of God in our lives.

The few years we had together—only six of them—unfolded gently and steadily, confirming the unity we had found together. They were years of shared in-depth studies and great companionship. We both made friends easily. We went to church with couples our age and even did some traveling. Our trip to Ohio to visit his family was especially meaningful.

There was no doubt our marriage was all in God's will and with his blessings. When Jim was diagnosed with final-stage renal disorder in 1996, there was grace in abundance to shepherd us through.

Intense dialysis was required and could be found in Loma Linda, world-renowned for its medical university and adjacent medical center. To facilitate the frequency and duration of these treatments, Jim and I moved to an independent senior-living complex near the hospital. The place is called Loma Linda Springs and is nestled on gentle hills with well-landscaped gardens. We had a two-bedroom apartment by the pool, which fit our needs well.

Loma Linda is adjacent to Redlands, where Nancy and Gary and their family lived; Nina and her children were not far away either. Jim's family lived in relatively nearby communities also, so together we were able to spend a good deal of time with both of our families. We found fellowship with other residents and even an excellent Bible study. Jim's home church was Plymouth Brethren, located in Riverside, close enough to attend regular services there.

He and I ate out a great deal. He found it a lively change, since his dialysis was so confining—two-and-a-half years of treatment, three times a week, each treatment four hours long. He had great patience and resolve, never complained, and his light sense of humor was always evident, smoothing the most anxious of times.

I can candidly say that even in these adverse circumstances, he was a joy to live with and care for. I loved him dearly—mainly for his steadfast, deep-spirited maturity and love of our Lord. We read the Bible daily—he, from the Old Testament; me, from the New. And we shared fervent prayers at meals, before bed, and with others who needed prayer.

Jim died peacefully in his sleep in 2000. His memorial service was sweet and reverent with both his family and mine joining to pay tribute to him. The next day, he was buried beside his first wife of many years at a mountain-top cemetery overlooking San Diego. Standing by me that day were Nina's two daughters, Natalie and Leilani. It meant a great deal to me that they were there.

On my own again, I was overwhelmed with the enormity of obligations. It dawned on me that trying to keep up with the individual lives of Jim's large family as well as those of my own was a pressure I could not handle without Jim. This was a distressing thought, so I prayed to the Lord. I met with Jim's family, expressed my feelings, and they understood. I was grateful for the God-given wisdom to do this and relieved that I would not be stretched too thin, both emotionally and physically.

We parted, each of us taking away with us the sweet memories of the last few years. Occasionally I do hear from one of Jim's relatives, and whenever that happens, it is all the more meaningful, as it is not done out of duty.

After Jim passed away, Nancy enthusiastically suggested that we go on a condo hunt for me in Redlands so that I could live closer to them. We soon found and negotiated for a fixer-upper at Fernwood, a gated community of condos with a large pool, tennis courts, and clubhouse.

Well—what a project that led to!

I was bound by a promise not to move in or even dare to see the condo again until invited. The plan was that the family would restore and decorate it according to their own particular talents in their time available. Nina, with her flair for design, conceptualized the transformation and made gorgeous drapes. From ceilings to floors, everything was fresh and upgraded. Nina, Nancy, Gary, and grandkids scrubbed, painted, hung pictures, and placed accessories.

Then one Saturday night I was royally escorted to see the breathtaking home that had been prepared for me. There was a fire blazing, music playing, and flowers everywhere. I gasped, overcome. And to think that this was my new home! I couldn't believe it was mine.

My time at Fernwood was a season of vitality and independence. I was single again and thriving—alone, yet never lonely. The Holy Spirit dwelled within me. Living for and through Christ was who I was and wanted to remain. With his strength I was strong, driving everywhere, and able to totally immerse myself in many activities open to me in the Redlands community. In addition to all of our family times, there was church and related outreach work, participation at Joslyn Senior Center, Republican Party support, bridge, and the refreshing stimulation of new associations. And as always, loyal friends from the past and I made sure to keep our connections open. Such ties are lifelong—loyalties unspoken, yet treasured.

In 2004, in the midst of this relaxed yet active time, devastating news struck our family. Nina's son Benjamin called to tell me he was taking his mother to the emergency room at Hoag Hospital in Newport Beach. We all knew she had not been feeling well for some time. Because of her Christian Science belief, she had avoided going to doctors, even though her kids, Nancy, Debby, and I had been urging her to get a checkup. By the time she agreed to see a doctor, matters had progressed to an acute state. I had to still my heart and accept that her religion was a big part of who she was.

In my mind, I see it all as a sad, rapid chain of events. The ER team identified advanced cancer and saw she was in crisis. She was taken into surgery. Then there we were in her hospital room, waiting to greet and love her when she came out of recovery. The room she had been assigned to was high up, overlooking the ocean. Somehow the majesty of that view was soothing to me. It tempered the shock of seeing her hooked up to a tangle of tubes and attached to all sorts of equipment.

Still, instinctively, my mother's heart wanted to rush to her side. I felt compelled to make sure she was comfortable and the blanket well tucked around her body. She looked so very cold. Reluctantly I deferred to the medical team buzzing professionally around her and focused on being grateful for their presence.

After her hospital stay, Nancy and Gary fixed a room for her in their home, with her furniture, to give her a place of comfort and support during her extended period of chemo— scheduled to begin right away. Nina wanted to have those treatments at Hoag, so we rotated as her drivers to take her from Redlands to Newport Beach three to five times a week.

The rides were complicated. We had to make sure to take proper food and equipment that might be needed en route, as sometimes Nina's reactions to the chemo were severe. Some weeks when I took her we stayed at the Embassy Suites in Costa Mesa, close to Hoag. Also for two weeks my niece, Michele, welcomed us to stay in her home on Lido Isle.

Nancy's organizational skills assured that every detail of Nina's care would be met while at home. She managed Nina's medicines, recording everything and being the go-between with her doctors. She also kept us each well-informed so we could do our very best for our patient. Nancy went home from a full workday to care for Nina in the evening and at night. While exhausting, their time together was precious.

The family pulled together, and we fit perfectly as a team. Most of my duties were at Nancy and Gary's. I would usually get there in the morning, fix breakfast and lunch for Nina, and then have dinner ready for everyone in the evening.

The household was kept lively and light, because there was no one there lacking wit. What a mercy it is to be able to laugh. Not only that, but Nina had the good fortune of four children and wonderful grandchildren. They came as often as they could—usually on the weekends. She took such delight in their faithful visits. Her youngest son, David, lived in Colorado, but he too came when he could. Debby also made many trips down from Red Bluff in Northern California to be with Nina.

In short, we each played our part in a united effort to care for our beloved Nina. Everybody spelled everybody, and each one gave moral support and cheer.

When Nina needed more assistance, a sweet nurse, Mindy, was added to the team. She became like one of the family. Her sense of humor and capable strength endeared her to us all.

Nina bore her suffering with qualities I had seen in my mother through her last illness. Neither of them complained; both retained their bubbly natures. I suspect that perhaps Nina reserved her more private feelings to share with her Christian Science practitioner, who stayed in frequent telephone contact with her from Pasadena. The practitioner would listen and talk to Nina and pray with her. They formed a strong bond that Nina held onto firmly. Another outlet for her inner thoughts was her habit of journaling.

My part in her last illness was less obvious. Naturally I sought every way possible to show my infinite mother's love for her. Yet inside I struggled, feeling inadequate to the task. One day it was just the two of us together. She was lying on the couch, resting with her eyes closed.

I let my agonized thoughts vent themselves silently, *Lord, my Nina, my baby, my beautiful grown daughter, my firstborn— she is dying! It's my turn, not hers!* I was bursting, ready to yell the words out loud in passionate anger.

Then unfathomable sadness trumped the anger. *She's going to you, Father. I am useless to stop it. What can I do? What can I say to her? I need your Holy Spirit desperately!*

Inside me there was a collapsing, drowning feeling, as though my repressed flood of tears had imploded. My eyes were dry by a fierce act of will.

Out of that place of despair I found myself reaching over to a side table. My Bible was there. I opened it and quietly turned the pages to the book of John. It is my favorite book in the Bible, filled with John's deep understanding of his dear friend, Jesus. In it he referred to himself as "the one whom Jesus loved." John tells us in detail of Jesus's last conversations with his apostles before he went to his death.

John was at that last supper table, laying his head against Jesus—perhaps in an effort to memorize his face, his voice, his words.

As I meditated on those things, I heard myself begin to read, starting with chapter 1, verse 1 of the Book of John: "In the beginning was the Word, and the Word was with God and the Word was God."

I looked over at Nina. Her eyes fluttered open. She was intently aware and intently listening.

I continued, "He was in the beginning with God. All things were made through him and without him nothing was made that was made" (John 1:2-3).

Not wanting to tire her, I was careful to check frequently to see if she might need me to stop. There was no such signal. Instead I saw only peace and serenity, whereas before, though resting, her expression had been strained. In moments when our eyes happened to meet, they joined in soft communion. So I continued. And so it went—all the way to the end of the book.

How my voice could have held out for that long is only a testimony to the Holy Spirit's strength in me. I did what God gave me to do. It was my prayer answered: I had comforted my daughter.

Heavenly Father, I shall thank you eternally. By showing me how to comfort her, I was comforted.

About five months into her stay at Nancy and Gary's, it was necessary to bring in hospice. Nina lived for four more months. Her last few days were quiet, and she was at peace. The night she passed away, Natalie, her oldest daughter, was there. Nancy and Gary were asleep, and I had gone home. All the family and Mindy came right away the next morning.

Nina's desire was to have a traditional Christian Science service at Pacific View Cemetery. The ceremony was very simple, held out on a grassy hillside. It was a bright sunny day, and we were overlooking the ocean that she loved.

I let my thoughts wander to the Nina I will always hold dear. I will ever see her as this picture portrays—a vibrant and beautiful young woman.

Slowly life returned to its normal pace. Yet, as it is when anyone of significance leaves our lives, normal must take on a new shape. So I resumed my schedule of activities. At one point I had a knee replacement, which was completely successful and interrupted the flow of my life only briefly. My leisurely yet active lifestyle continued enjoyably for a number of years, until I noticed that some things were not quite as easily done as they had been.

A subtle, very gradual physical weakness began to tap me gently on the shoulder. I wondered if it would be smart to consider another living situation that would lighten my load of physical errands, such as grocery shopping, cleaning, and cooking for myself. I wondered if moving to a senior living facility, while I was relatively active and capable, made sense.

More and more often those questions in my mind got an affirmative answer, so I talked the idea over with my girls. It wasn't long before we began a concerted search for my next home, which led me to "Gracious Retirement Living" at Mission Commons in Redlands. The year was 2010. I was eighty-seven—not too old for more adventure.

Chapter 10

MISSION COMMONS

Reflections

So here I am at Mission Commons, my chosen home. It is a lovely place where an assortment of interesting seniors share their lives. The architectural concept for this place could be that of a luxury liner. When we sit at our tables in the vast dining room, the view easily enables the imagination to conjure an ocean voyage—certainly a good metaphor for my own life. From this vantage point I have been able to recall my journey, indulging myself in memory. I can truthfully say with satisfaction that it has been a great trip—and it's not over yet!

Since moving here, I no longer have to concern myself with obtaining the necessities of life. They are provided for me. Food is shopped for, and good meals are prepared and served; housekeeping is automatic; assistance is only a buzzer away; even the beauty parlor is in-house.

And my thoughtful family is ever in touch with me. Nancy lives the closest, so she sees me often and blesses me with her presence, her concern, and the little things of life that I didn't even realize I needed.

I did not expect that another benefit of this time in my life would be that my loved ones no longer need me. Thank God that even my grandchildren are now self-sufficient, healthy, smart adults, for that allows me to sit back and savor the news of their lives and enjoy their visits.

Leisure hours spent in Nancy and Gary's comfortable back yard, talking with family and friends, are cherished times.

Those one-on-one times are really the best for me now. I find that the larger scale gatherings, which were part and parcel of my life when I was younger, need to be a bit shorter and less often now. It is not easy to keep up with the great-grands, for they grow up so fast that their little faces take on new character each time I see them. A wonder of God, surely, but challenging to the great-grandmother who finds it illusive to keep track of who is who and whose is whose.

However, I must relate one spectacular, large gathering. Unbeknownst to me, my girls and their kids had concocted the idea of a surprise birthday party for me to which all the extended family would be invited. Not only were they invited, but they came—in droves.

From my point of view, my ninetieth was a landmark I hoped to ignore by casually stepping over it. There was, however, an event I wanted to attend that coincided with the day. The Lei'd Back Bunch, a ukulele musical group that Nancy and some friends started some years ago, would be performing at the Lutheran Church at one o'clock. I was looking forward to it, and I was on time.

Entering the big hall, I saw the musicians on the stage ahead and noticed the room full of colorfully decorated round tables. I couldn't avoid regretfully noticing that there were very few in attendance. I was led to a seat at a front table, facing the smiling faces of the ukulele strummers who were already lightheartedly singing "You Are My Sunshine." Behind me I heard a few footsteps entering, then more footsteps.

Finally, I thought with relief, *some more in the audience.*

The singing got louder and happier. As chairs scraped, being drawn up to tables, Nancy emceed a big welcome greeting to all. The "all" turned out to be friends and family members—many of whom I hadn't seen for ages. There were nieces, nephews, children of all sizes, and close friends. Altogether there were about one hundred dear ones.

Then suddenly two words rang out: "Happy Birthday!" followed by "Surprise!"

I gasped for air, tears welling up. Each person came by with kisses galore. Nancy announced that the family had come from near and far. My grandson, Robert, had even come unexpectedly all the way from Japan.

Family pictures and memorabilia were posted along a big side wall. Delicious gourmet canapés, artistically arranged, were brought to each table. The service staff was made up entirely of darling family children—some touchingly shy but with gleaming eyes, some totally into the part with the broadest of smiles.

Nancy's narrative included many meaningful and funny stories, hitting highlights of my life. She built drama and entertainment into her tales by seamlessly interweaving songs appropriate to each era—all rendered by the wonderful Lei'd Back Bunch. And several of the children made up a routine to "Side by Side," just as Nina, Nancy, and I had done for Bob when we met him on Guam.

Various family members went forward to give stirring tributes to me and share their memories. Of course, many of these stories included Bob and Nolan, my beloved brother. Nolan had recently passed away and was very much missed that day. Our lives had been so close over the years—spiced with lively opinions, ups and downs, and ins and outs—and throughout we had remained best buddies. How he would have loved this day of recaptured times, tender tears, and joyful laughter.

I was and am grateful with all my heart, for certainly God was present in that room. There is no doubt every single person felt a powerful, undeniable force—the silver thread of love binding and blending us in unity.

In this senior community of Mission Commons, I am struck by the fact that all of us who live here are winding down. The nearness of our end is an unstated yet loud fact. Our management staff are dedicated to making each day interesting. Many groups come to entertain. Events are planned and anticipated. Holiday traditions are celebrated.

However, when I moved here, I found a missing component. There was no group of believers who gathered to worship God and seek him. The designated chapel was no more than a bare room with a few chairs.

Gradually, I encouraged a group of interested believers to meet there consistently and study the Word together.

The chapel has slowly been transformed into a room for meditation, study, and prayer. Each of us has contributed a bit by adding inspiring pictures and other uplifting touches. A large cross of beautifully carved wood is the focal point.

I also have my own private chapel in my apartment. My prayer chair occupies a corner of my bedroom next to my regular reading companions—my Bible, favorite devotionals, and current reading material. Each morning I pray and sense the Holy Spirit's presence with me, conscious of his leading me daily in the ways he wills me to go. My gratitude is deep, real, and sincere for all God's provisions. Praise is continually on my lips.

Talking about the chapel in Mission Commons reminds me of my close friend, Millie, who donated the piano/organ for the chapel. Millie was already living here when I moved in. We clicked immediately, learning we had many, many things in common—even the same birthday in 1923. We felt like sisters who had been bonded from birth.

We were tablemates with three other compatible ladies in our dining room and enjoyed referring to ourselves as the Fabulous Five. We depended on each other to team up in group activities, like competitive poker. What a great sadness it was for our group—but particularly for Millie and me—when Millie became ill. We both knew that it was her final illness.

Thank you, Lord, for providing fellowship for me throughout my life, friends willing to share joys and hardships. No value can be placed on that gift. It is priceless.

Not too long before Millie's death, I began to work on this—my life story. I took my time because I now trusted God to guide my ways when I acknowledge him. I sensed an almost audible encouragement: "Come to me. Pray, and I will give you answers and direction."

With those words in mind, I took full advantage of the ample time I have had to myself—time to reflect in mind, memory, and spirit, with no physical restraints or practical demands to distract me. Much of what I wrote came so easily that I felt it was inspired, almost as if God were the author.

Now—four years and many memories later—the book is finished. I have recounted my journey and family roots that were so lovingly planted.

That is, I thought it was finished.

But four experiences came to me very strongly one night, demanding to be written. Why did these four images appear to me so vividly and insistently, just as I was completing the book? Was there something else I needed to learn or say?

*

The first memory was of our sailing/boating days. We would call out excitedly, "Cast off and let's go!" It was our rallying cry for fun and adventure. We set the sails just so, and when we caught the wind, there was a feeling of exuberance, of soaring in its might.

*

Then I remembered night sailing under the vast black skies studded with countless heavenly stars. We would set our sights on the brilliant North Star, an ever-faithful guide. We knew with surety that it would lead us home.

*

Third, I remembered times flying over the jungles of Laos and Thailand when the pilot—in spite of threatening black thunderheads—would aim for a tiny patch of light, a clearing in the clouds, barely enough to guide his small plane between the black masses to safe landing.

*

I realize now that throughout my life, whether I was aware of it or not, like the wind in our sails, God has been powerfully supporting and propelling me. I see that God has been a constant and consistent reference point, like the North Star, always there if I paid attention. And just like the pilot in dark storms, I have had free will to turn toward the light amidst life's difficulties.

*

Lastly, I remembered flying east on a huge airliner from the dark night of the west. I looked out my window to a radiant, gorgeous sight—the magnificence of dawn seen from thousands of feet above the earth. The curve of the earth was rimmed by the rising sun becoming brighter minute by minute. How small I felt as I observed the tiny shadow of our plane on a distant cloud. For hours the constant hum of the engines surrounded me. I remember feeling secure in the pilot's capable hands.

*

From my perspective of ninety-three years, I know that I have been living within the cocoon of God's loving grace, a tiny speck in the massive universe of time and dimension, securely transported through the nights and days of my life by my personal pilot.

*

The compelling visions became a part of me until I captured with fullness and clarity the wisdom and importance of their messages—and I saw that my journey has, indeed, been charted after all.

My next adventure is a sure thing, for I know who is in control. Departure will be signaled when I hear my Navigator call,

"Cast off, Sue, and let's go!"

Epilogue

As a teenager I was moved to write poetry,
unaware of the events to come,
yet aware on some level . . .

An urge, a tormenting, burning urge
To live with splendorous lands.
Do they exist? I could not know!
My home is my globe
My dreams are my maps.
But my heart beats the life
Of those splendorous lands.

Somehow, no place except Heav'n itself
Contains such glory as these tales unfold
They build up hope, they illumine life.
Cruel propaganda to youth!

I will conquer that urge with swords of truth!
With the will of God, and love of man.
And gaiety, my steamer, will make
rough waters smooth.

Written 1938

Suzzanne

An urge, a tormenting, burning urge
To live with splendorous lands.
Do they exist?   I could not know!
My home is my globe
My dreams are my maps.
But my heart desires the life
Of those splendorous lands.

Somehow, no place except Heav'n itself
Contains such glory as these tales unfold
They build up hope, they illumine life.
Cruel propaganda to youth!

I will conquor that urge with words of truth
With the will of God, and love of men,
And gaity, my steamer, will make
            rough waters smooth.

Written 1938

What will I do
When I become too old
To enjoy all of this
Glorious youth?

It is so important
So vital to one's entire life
To grasp, to hold it
Dear to him.

Good may come, bad may come
But to be able to take all
In your stride, to be able to laugh
Ah, then youth is dear.

Written '39

Suzzanne

What will I do
when I become too old
To enjoy all of this
Glorious youth?

It is so important
So vital to one's entire life
To grasp, to hold it
Dear to him.

Good may come, bad may come
But to be able to take all
In your stride, to be able to laugh,
Oh, then youth is dear.

Written '39.

I am calm, grateful, content—yet
I feel in me, rising, building up ready to burst—
A new mood.
That mood is the sum of my experience added up
It will bring the supreme expression of love.

These fifteen years of my short life
Seem but a day right now.
Really they are just one day
One moment of time
And all of this moment is the expression of love.

Ah, if when I become more versed, more wise
Can only teach to one person or the universe
That such a feeling is an eternal one,
For we are born and die as that expression of love.

Written 1938–'39

Suzzanne

I am calm, grateful, content --- yet
I feel in me, rising, bubbling up
    ready to burst --
A new mood.
That mood is the sum of my experiences
    added up
It will bring the supreme expression
    of love.

These fifteen years of my short life
Seem but a day right now,
Really they are just one day
One moment of time
And all of this moment is the ex-
    pression of love.

Oh, if when I become more versed,
    more wise
Can only teach to one person or
    the universe
That such a feeling is an eternal
    one,
For we are born and die as that
    expression of love

Written 1938-'39

Sue welcomes emails at
sdabcat@gmail.com

Or visit her webpage at
suedabneycatalano.com

Ariel Hollender, Sue's scribe, can be reached at
LivingWaterScribe@gmail.com